WESTMAR COLLE □ **W9-BVH-171**

THE COMMONWEALTH AND INTERNATIONAL LIBRARY

Joint Chairmen of the Honorary Editorial Advisory Board

SIR ROBERT ROBINSON, O.M., F.R.S., LONDON

DEAN ATHELSTAN SPILHAUS, MINNESOTA

Publisher: ROBERT MAXWELL, M.C., M.P.

LIBERAL STUDIES DIVISION

General Editors: D. F. BRATCHELL, E. F. CANDLIN

Science and Starvation

AN INTRODUCTION TO ECONOMIC DEVELOPMENT

Science and Starvation

AN INTRODUCTION TO ECONOMIC DEVELOPMENT

by

DONALD J. HUGHES

PERGAMON PRESS

OXFORD · LONDON · EDINBURGH · NEW YORK
TORONTO · SYDNEY · PARIS · BRAUNSCHWEIG

Pergamon Press Ltd., Headington Hill Hall, Oxford
4 & 5 Fitzroy Square, London W.1
Pergamon Press (Scotland) Ltd., 2 & 3 Teviot Place, Edinburgh 1
Pergamon Press Inc., 44–01 21st Street, Long Island City, New York 11101
Pergamon of Canada Ltd., 207 Queen's Quay West, Toronto 1
Pergamon Press (Aust.) Pty. Ltd., 19a Boundary Street,
Rushcutters Bay, N.S.W. 2011, Australia
Pergamon Press S.A.R.L., 24 rue des Écoles, Paris 5e
Vieweg & Sohn GmbH, Burgplatz 1, Braunschweig

Printed in Great Britain by A. Wheaton & Co., Exeter

Contents

List of Maps and Charts

List of Photographs

Synopsis

prepared plans for its development. A time scale of decades—construction held up by lack of money and unsettled political conditions.

X. *Trade not Aid.*

Aid can be wiped out by adverse terms of trade. U.N. Trade Conferences of 1964 and 1968 urged developed countries to help by giving favourable trading terms to have-nots.

XI. *The Population Problem.*

World population will double in thirty-five years. Trends in population growth—changes are slow to take effect. The theory of Malthus—is he right? The need for both food and population policies.

XII. *The Development Decade.*

The United Nations names the 1960's as "Development Decade". Plans for action to achieve target rate of growth. Survey of decade at midpoint shows targets not being reached. U Thant shows that potential is there.

XIII. *Back to People.*

The need for changes in ideas and minds. Poverty breeds apathy. Development a single process in which everything must go forward together. India's Community Development scheme; Japanese workers and industrialisation. The need for those in developed countries to understand problems.

Introduction

by F. D. FLOWER, Principal, Kingsway College for Further Education

IT is a commonplace of the 1960's to say that the development of modern communications has reduced the size of the world. It is perhaps trite to comment on the man-made satellites encircling earth and moon and the spacemen crawling out of their capsules for their walk in space and to draw a moral about the contraction of the planet we live on and its fundamental unity. Unfortunately the cynic, by way of contrast, can point to the man-made obstacles to free communication, the uncrossable frontiers, and the intractable political problems that still divide the shrunken globe.

In this context it becomes depressingly easy to complain that our current essay in regulating the affairs of the world, the United Nations, has like its predecessor, the League of Nations, revealed itself at best a failure, at worst a fraud. The apparent inability of the United Nations to bring about a peaceful solution to the war in Vietnam, the hesitancy of Great Britain in bringing the Rhodesian dispute to the judgement of the Security Council, the protracted confrontation of Israel and her Arab neighbours all lend colour to this view of international politics.

But it is also true that the world can only solve those problems that it wishes to solve *as a world*, that is as a united community. A consensus is necessary, a clear agreement on the need to act and a willingness to act. The real political achievement of the United Nations is not to be measured by the absence of universally accepted solutions, but by the inescapable fact that its presence has prevented or limited conflict and marked out the profiles of the more difficult dilemmas that still await resolution.

There is fortunately another approach which promises ultimately far more success in guaranteeing international peace and security than any stroke of political genius, or sequence of hard bargaining at the conference table, or any juggling with the balance of military power. And it is with certain aspects of this alternative, perhaps less glamorous approach, that this book is concerned.

The ultimate solution lies in learning to work together on the common problems of all men and which all nations recognise as important to them. We must come to realise that the granting of a constitution does not make a democracy, however progressive the constitution. Men have to live together and to work together for at least a minimum of common ends to make it possible for the will of the majority to prevail without destruction of the rights of minorities, and for minorities to learn to accept majority decisions loyally.

In the world today, in spite of political divisions that may dominate the headlines, there are numerous problems, great and small, that involve all countries. Finding answers to these many problems is beyond the power of any state, however large and affluent, and therefore in their own interests nation states are having to co-operate. By working together, often no doubt in a partial and piecemeal fashion, the nations of the world will eventually learn to live together in such a way that none will represent a threat to any other. In this functional approach to an ultimate unified world, the specialised agencies of the United Nations and its various programmes and perspectives such as that of the Development Decade have probably a more decisive part to play than its more obvious peacekeeping activities. In the history books a hundred years hence river projects in the Mekong and Jordan valleys may be regarded as far more important than the wars fought in their neighbourhoods. Already today we are learning that it is to the advantage of no man or of no nation that another man or another nation should live in poverty and hunger. Their rescue is not charity but an act of self-interest.

For helping to remind us of this perspective Dr. Hughes's book is to be commended. At a time of some frustration when, though so much is possible, we are distracted by the complications of international politics, this book is a salutary reminder that our current preoccupations are with superficial difficulties and the real problems lie below. It is not enough to be aware that the interests of all will be served by the economic development of all. The nature of the process of development itself, how it has happened in the past and how it can be extended and accelerated in the present and future needs to be widely understood, as much in the developed as in the developing countries. This book is a notable contribution to this understanding. Its fund of information is a guide to the intricacies of the interrelated problems of food, population and economic development all the world over. It should prove invaluable for teachers, especially those engaged in liberal studies in further and higher education, and for all serious students of this aspect of international relations.

Preface

THIS book covers a very wide range of topics in a short space, and some explanation of its purpose may be helpful.

In 1961 the United Nations launched the Development Decade, with the idea of drawing attention to the increasing scale of international co-operation in the development of human and material resources throughout the world, and the need for a yet much greater effort if the burden of world poverty is to be lightened, and the rapidly increasing population of this planet is even to maintain its present entirely inadequate standard of living, let alone improve this to a level consistent with human dignity and civilisation.

This Decade is drawing to a close with many of its targets far from achieved; yet the problem of development becomes every year more clearly a fundamental subject for anyone interested in the social studies or current affairs. To understand its implications needs a very broadly-based knowledge which to many of us can only be somewhat superficial and general, but which can also form the foundation of an intellectual discipline to those who are led that way.

This book attempts to meet this particular need. It is hoped that it can be read with profit by any student or young man or woman with an interest in the world they live in. That world is essentially a dynamic world in which technological progress forms one of the main motive forces to human action, but alongside people's interest in scientific and technical advance mercifully goes a very real concern and shame for the intolerable differences of the human condition which exist in this twentieth-century world—a concern which is exemplified by the widespread support for such bodies as Oxfam and War on Want, and by the often unsatisfied desire of very large numbers of young people to undertake some form of voluntary service overseas.

It is hoped that many of such young people who want to understand a little more fully the issues which lie behind this human situation will be helped if they read this book; and that any such student, but more particularly the scientists and technologists in training, may be able to see more clearly the relevance of their future life's work to the great movement of humanity which is now under way.

But because of the tremendous span of the subject this book can only be the briefest of introductions. For this reason it has also been designed in the hope that it might serve as the basis and framework for a deeper and fuller course of study which might be undertaken by groups concerned with social studies—particularly as part of a liberal studies course in colleges of technology or in sixth forms. This could be carried out at almost any level of depth required, and could concentrate as desired on any particular aspect of the subject. (For example, the shortage of space has meant that in this book the problems of the underdeveloped countries have been dealt with generally, and more particularly from the standpoint of the international aid required; but perhaps one of the most illuminating and useful studies which could arise out of the general theme would be a comparison of, for example, the problems of India in the present and future with those of the U.S.A. or U.S.S.R. in the past.)

In such liberal studies courses the book would be a base from which to work. Each chapter covers a main topic, and concludes with suggestions for further study and reading. This can be carried out as part of a fuller course, or as individual student projects.

By its nature the subject involves an exploration of what technology really is, of its function in the developed world, and of the sort of role which technologists of all kinds will be playing both in the developed countries and also in assistance to the underdeveloped in the next ten, twenty and thirty years. By extension this becomes also a matter of concern for scientists, even of the "pure" variety; and of course it raises, as anyone should realise, issues of great importance for social scientists of all persuasions.

A list of books which will assist those who wish to make this study in greater depth is appended at the end of each chapter.

PART I

Introductory

CHAPTER 1

The Scientific Revolution and the Starving Millions

It has been said that the progress of man is the history of his technological advances—from the primitive, flint-striking Stone Age man to the computer-using expert of the twentieth century.

It has also been said that science—i.e. physical science—has outstripped politics, which is the science, or art, of living together; and that if science stood still for seventy-five years politics would not catch up with it.

Both of these statements, and not least the second, contain much truth. That we have "progressed" to the mastery of atomic energy is a measure of the first; that we still threaten to blow ourselves to pieces as a result is a pitiful commentary on the second. In another direction the paradox is equally striking.

We live, we say, in a scientific and technological age, where the machines of an industrialised society pour out in profusion goods of all kinds for our satisfaction. Yet in this very age over half of the human race suffers from malnutrition, disease, even starvation. What is the sense of calling this a "scientific and technological age"? Does the Indian peasant, planting his rice seeds by hand on his little plot as his ancestors have done for centuries, regard himself as living in a technological age? Does the Bolivian villager who can neither read nor write consider himself as the heir to the scientific revolution of modern times?

More and more young men and women from this country and the other developed countries of the West are taking into the world today with their trained minds and technical resources a power

3

which is quite momentous in its possible effects on human affairs. They can make use of their abilities in many diverse ways. An increasing number of them will certainly find themselves with opportunities of service overseas in which a knowledge of the problems facing the poorer countries will be of the first importance.

This book sets out to answer a number of the questions which must be asked by those students and others who are concerned not only to acquire knowledge but also to know what the effect of that knowledge and its application is likely to be on society. Or, rather, it sets out to discuss these questions in a way which will enable the reader himself to form his own conclusions; for in the social sciences, which are the study of human behaviour, there are no direct answers to questions as there are in the physical sciences. In the social sciences, for example, you can ask "What is the effect on children of violence in television westerns?"; but you cannot get a precise answer, because one child is different from another, because the human mind cannot be analysed in its causal sequences as can physical matter; and for many other similar reasons.

And if you delve into the future and ask "What will the effect of atomic power be on the world?" you pose a question to which the answer is even more unpredictable. It is unpredictable because on the individual and collective decisions of men rests the eventual answer; and each one of us helps to make these decisions. Therefore, the very asking of the question and the discussion of the issues involved of themselves affect the solution; because such questioning and discussion affect the decisions and policies of men acting as individuals or in communities.

This difference between the nature of the physical and the social sciences is a principal reason for the backward state of politics, which results in the fact that we have so far made such limited use of technology in the world as a whole. Men like to be able to have a definite answer to the questions they ask, and although modern scientific thought, with its probability theories and its hinting at dark uncertainties behind the apparently unchangeable order of the physical universe, is no longer so unequivocal in its answers as it used to be, we still feel much more certain that water will turn into steam at a temperature of 100°C than we do about the result of the next general election.

Scientists and technologists must always realise this essential difference between the two studies. All valid answers in politics or economics are relative to conditions at the time those answers are given; and the quest for the good society, for the world in which men and women can live out their lives in freedom from want and fear, goes on eternally. Its frontiers expand ever more widely as do those of the physical sciences; and it is a land in which Robert Louis Stevenson's claim that it is better to travel than to arrive must always be true; because you will never finally arrive.

The study of economic development, and particularly that of today's underdeveloped countries, must range over a number of branches of social studies. One may begin with a consideration of the unscientific society of today—that is, with a look at the poorer countries of the world with a view to discovering the nature of their poverty. One can then consider the areas of prosperity to discover why it is that they, and not others, are prosperous. These studies will involve a certain amount of geography and quite a bit of economic history. When one turns to the question of how the underdeveloped countries can emulate their richer brothers and move towards a decent standard of living for their citizens, some economic theory is involved. And the whole matter is from first to last bound up with politics and political decisions of the highest importance.

But precisely because one can so easily get lost in academic discussions on the way, we should always remember that the subject of all social study is man. And not "Man" with a capital M, but little men with little "m"s. The illiterate Moroccan weaver whose children cannot go to school because the dilapidated hut which serves as a school accommodates twenty in a village of three thousand; the woman in Greece who has to climb two miles up and down a mountain slope in all weathers several times a day to fetch water from a well because there is no supply in the village; and the British student who is about to pass out from a university or college of technology with a skill and know-how in economics or in building or in mechanical engineering. These are the subjects of our study; none of them is an island, all of them are part of the main. All are involved in the other, in humanity.

So we may start by looking at the two-thirds of the human race who, according to U.N. statistics, are underdeveloped. What are their characteristics? Where do they live? How do they live?

Further Study

Those who wish to consider further the essential differences between the nature and the techniques of the physical and social sciences should read a simple introduction to sociology, political science or economics.

The Science of Society, by J. Rumney and J. Maier (Duckworth), is an introduction to the meaning of the social sciences in general.

CHAPTER 2

The Nature of Poverty

THE main characteristics of an underdeveloped country are well summarised by Paul Hoffman, the Administrator of the U.N. Development Programme, in his booklet *One Hundred Countries, One and One Quarter Billion People*:

"Everyone knows an underdeveloped country when he sees one. It is a country characterised by poverty, with beggars in the cities, and villagers eking out a bare subsistence in the rural areas. It is a country lacking in factories of its own, usually with inadequate supplies of power and light. It usually has insufficient roads and railroads, insufficient government services, poor communications. It has few hospitals, and few institutions of higher learning. Most of its people cannot read or write. In spite of the generally prevailing poverty of the people, it may have isolated islands of wealth, with a few persons living in luxury. Its banking system is poor; small loans have to be obtained through money lenders who are often little better than extortionists. Another striking characteristic of an underdeveloped country is that its exports to other countries usually consist almost entirely of raw materials, ores or fruits or some staple product with possibly a small admixture of luxury handicrafts. Often the extraction or cultivation of these raw material exports is in the hands of foreign companies.

"Some of these underdeveloped countries are new. Others of the underdeveloped countries, oddly enough, are among the oldest known to history and were the seats of refined and elaborate cultures while Europe was in a state of barbarism and America was yet undiscovered. In some of these ancient centres of culture, such as India and China, there is reason to believe that the life of the average man is worse than it was centuries ago. To-day in these countries population has increased to such an extent that the ancient methods of agriculture and handicraft can no longer provide adequate food and goods to meet even basic needs."

This is a cogent summary. It would be as well to analyse it a little more closely.

First of all—the nature of poverty. This is, clearly, the fundamental characteristic that we all recognise, and which is common to
all areas of underdevelopment. People are poor; and they are poor
not just in the sense that they have no money in their pockets. They
are poor because they do not have enough to eat, because their
health is bad through inadequate diet or inadequate shelter or
sanitation; and if you ask why they do not have adequate sanitation
the short answer is because they do not have enough to eat; consequently their whole life is taken up with a struggle to gain from the
land a subsistence for themselves and their families. Because their
health is bad they are not efficient as farmers and peasants, and so
their efforts to grow more food are unsuccessful. And because they
are hungry and ill and absorbed with the daily struggle for food
they cannot build schools or factories or hospitals. This is the vicious
circle which we shall meet again.

Those who have not seen it sometimes find it difficult to imagine
the real meaning of poverty of this kind. A couple of pen-pictures
may help.

Firstly, from *The Fever Peaks*, by Wayne Mineau:

"Halfway up the hill we overtook a slow-moving caravan of travellers.
It was a Nepalese family of seven making its way to the capital—a father
and *his* father, a wife, her sister, and three children in their teens. The older
man, who had a wheezing cough that gave him obvious distress as he toiled
back-bent through the rocks and rubble, was using a length of sugar cane
as a staff for support, and every few minutes when the coughing eased he
took a bite out of the top: energy, from a walking stick, as well as lubrica-
tion for his dried old mouth.

"Ahead of him walked two girls, one with the fat legs of filaria. The third
child was a boy of about fourteen who was helping his father in the most
harrowing example of porterage I had yet seen. Inside the cane basket on the
father's back was a woman, her legs and arms dangling over the sides, her
head slumped forward. She was all the time making a falsetto moaning
noise, a vibrating wail as the basket went jerking over the track. Whenever
the path became especially steep or marked by high stepping-stones of rock,
the boy would stand behind his father to take some of the weight of the
basket on one shoulder. Carrying a ragged cloth bundle that looked as if it
contained the family's chattels, the man's wife walked at the front of the
column.

"At my behest Govind Man Singh got into conversation with the woman and we learned that they were carrying her sister to a doctor, or maybe the hospital, at Katmandu. From the wife's description it sounded as if the sister were dying of TB, but the urgency of their trip lay in the fact that she had been badly burned, a few days earlier, when an oil lamp overturned in a village rest house where they had spent a night. This was the fourth day of their slow trek to the capital. . . .

"Till then I had not given a thought to problems such as *how* you got yourself into medical care if you fell critically ill in some remote hamlet of the hills, miles and days from the capital. This, it seemed, was the answer, a basket cradle on a man's breaking back."

And now some short extracts from a medical missionary's experiences in Nyasaland (Electra Dory, *Leper Country*).

"The shacks were devoid of light, fresh air entered through the crevices. The people ate and slept on the floor. Their possessions were the three essentials for life, a water vessel, a cooking pot and a flat basket. The wealthier owned a hoe and a sleeping mat and perhaps a few shreds of covering—the filthy frayed remnant could not be described as a blanket. . . .

"On the whole the dirtiness of the population was of an earthy nature. They all lived in close contact with the soil. It was their bed—their chairs, their table—how could they avoid being dusty and coated with particles? Those who lived near water enjoyed washing, but when the source of water was a tiny hole a mile or so away—well, who could blame them for omitting their ablutions? . . .

"This event was followed by an epidemic of premature babies, and we were seldom without a tiny creature. With the single exception of one half of a twin, all survived the critical first month. . . . It was disappointing to learn that many died later, often when they had reached normal weight and were making progress. Malaria, pneumonia and whooping cough, as well as unwise feeding and the native drugs, were all available for the decimation of the infant population. . . .

"Hunger, hunger. It was the sole topic of conversation. Bare subsistence was their perennial lot, now they were faced with starvation. They burrowed under the trees for succulent roots thereby aiding the soil erosion. But how could one forbid this grovelling as they cried piteously for food?

"Thousands owed their lives to the Government, which took prompt action to import maize; only the weak and aged succumbed."

But the problem of economic development is in no way one which can be met simply by an idealistic charitable urge in response to horror stories or photographs. It is a major operation requiring a high degree of political and economic skill and the enlistment of a very high proportion of the technological and social wisdom of the world.

To each expert the facts of the human condition may appear in a different form. The statistician may see them in terms of income per head in the different countries of the world.

The average income per head in the U.S.A. is $3000 per annum. In India it is just over $70.

Put in another way, just over two-thirds of the world's population (67 per cent), living in the undeveloped countries, share 15 per cent, less than one-sixth, of the world's income.

Such figures of national income undoubtedly exaggerate the difference between rich and poor. For example, prices vary enormously between one country and another, and for the equivalent of an American dollar one can get far more in Bangkok or Delhi than in New York. Moreover, the whole of an advanced country's economy is geared to money-as-a-medium-of-exchange, and almost everything we obtain we have to pay for. But in an African village most of the bare necessities of life may be produced by the family in the home and not enter into the circle of money exchange. Nevertheless, the differences are so tremendous that this proviso does not seriously affect the issue.

If anyone is still in doubt there are other statistics which can in no way be explained away.

"In countries such as China, Egypt and India, where the average expectation of life is in the neighbourhood of thirty years, only 54 out of every 100 children born ever reach the age of 15" (Calder, *Medicine and Man*).

In the U.S.A. at the mid-century the mean life expectancy figures were 65 for males and 71 for females.

In India in 1956 only 31 million children were receiving any school education—less than 40 per cent of the whole.

In North America, Western Europe and the U.S.S.R. there is generally one doctor for fewer than 1000 inhabitants compared with one for 32,000 in Afghanistan, 39,000 in Mali and 96,000 in Ethiopia.

But even statistics of this kind do not give the full picture; per-

haps the least fully appreciated fact is that the gap between the advanced and the undeveloped countries is increasing steadily.
In this country we are constantly being reminded of the need for increased productivity, and our long-term economic planning is

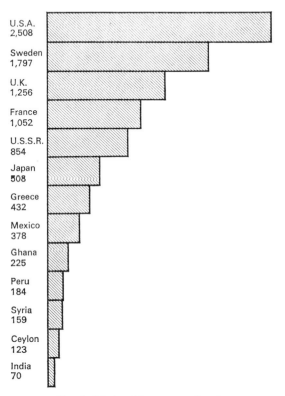

U.S.A.
2,508

Sweden
1,797

U.K.
1,256

France
1,052

U.S.S.R.
854

Japan
508

Greece
432

Mexico
378

Ghana
225

Peru
184

Syria
159

Ceylon
123

India
70

FIG. 1. National income per head.

based on the achievement of a rate of growth not far removed from $3\frac{1}{2}$ or 4 per cent per annum. It is indeed argued strongly that this country will forfeit its position as one of the leading industrial and commercial powers if anything less is achieved. Such an advance would double the national income in less than twenty years.

The underdeveloped countries, too, are increasing their total national income. But at the most optimistic estimate their annual rate of increase is no more than 3 per cent. And their population is growing at a much faster rate than is ours.

Put in another way, during the 1950's the industrialised countries were able to increase income *per head* at a rate of 2½ per cent per annum, while the less developed countries could only manage an annual rate of 1 per cent.

At this rate the hungry African will never catch up. At this rate it will be seventy years before *he* doubles his standard of living—and at £25 per year even to double his income won't make him rich.

The social scientist or economist who studies the characteristics of underdevelopment will look not only at the individual's basic needs but at those of the community. He will find that many things which we take for granted in our society are absent, and he knows that these things are a necessary condition of a higher standard of living and a modern civilised community. He knows that our own state would perish without them.

If you question a thoughtful and intelligent African or Indian on the subject, he will probably name education as the first of those enriching gifts for which he envies the advanced nations. If we, in Great Britain, in the U.S.A. and the U.S.S.R., see a great increase in educational facilities, particularly in higher education, as the condition for the maintenance of our respective competitive places in the world and of our continued economic growths, how much more does the African worship this wealth-giving god of whom he has seen so little?

The absence of schools and universities is one sign of the impoverished community; but there are many others.

One of the first truths a student of elementary economics learns about our own society is our extreme dependence one on another. None of us lives a self-sufficient life economically; we depend on others for our food, our homes, our clothing, and in return we do some service for them.

The only way in which it is possible for such a system to work efficiently is by the use of some form of token for exchange; and

PLATE 1. Poverty and disease. This French Cameroons "banana village" is built into a swamp, an ideal breeding ground for mosquitoes. (By courtesy of United Nations.)

PLATE 2. The common lot of half humanity today and in the past. This seventh-century sculpture from Southern India shows a man suffering from hunger. (By courtesy of United Nations.)

PLATE 3. Medical science as she was. Compounding and distilling a balsam. (A broadside from the collection of the Society of Antiquaries, London.)

PLATE 4. Transport old: the original London–Bath mail coach. (By courtesy of H.M. Postmaster General.)

PLATE 5. Transport new: how the car has altered cities. Freeways in Detroit. (By courtesy of the United States Information Service.)

PLATE 6. The largest city in the world, Tokyo, has all the hallmarks of a modern industrialised community. (By courtesy of United Nations.)

the advanced countries have developed a very intricate system based on money to do this job for them. Our economy not only could not function without money; a great deal of the impetus towards the development of industry and trade comes directly from the financial mechanisms which we have contrived through banks, finance houses, hire purchase firms and the like.

Very little of this complex exists in the underdeveloped countries. Much of life there consists, as it has always done in primitive communities, of peasants eking out a subsistence living from their own local patch of soil. In such conditions, money has little place; there is nothing much to buy with it if you have it. And a characteristic of the undeveloped economy is the absence of banks, of all that mechanism of credit, and of facilities for savings which lie behind the great expansive economic surges of the West.

These refinements of our advanced civilisation are not without their very considerable drawbacks. Apart from the moralist's view of money (or the love of it) as the root of all evil, we are only too aware that money can be a very awkward commodity to handle, and its misuse may lead to unemployment or to inflation or to an aggravation of inequalities between classes. Nevertheless, a financial structure which provides for the possibilities of investment, of widespread credit facilities and of capital accumulation is essential to economic growth.

Let us next consider what Hoffman calls "insufficient government services".

Though there is a tendency in this country to treat the civil servant as one of the butts of the modern world—the little bureaucrat with his careful filing system for passing responsibility on to the next department—such a picture is quite misleading in general terms. Our society would be quite unable to function without both the trained administrators capable of bringing their judicial minds to the impartial consideration of problems on which the Government must make important decisions, and also the operators at a lower level who keep the public sector going—the post office clerks and engineers, the health officials, the factory inspectors. All these presuppose a state with both reasonable educational facilities and also the resources to spare a quite large proportion of its working population for "services" rather than for the production of basic commodities such as food and clothing.

One of the favourite projects of Dag Hammarskjöld, U.N. Secretary-General from 1953 to 1961, was for the formation by the United Nations of a pool of expert public administrators who would be available to advise member nations and to help them both in the taking of wise decisions on their development policies and also in planning for the provision of the corps of public servants which they would need. The Congo offers a glaring example of what happens to a country given its independence at a time when no attempts of any kind had been made to equip it with trained administrators and specialists.

Along with the question of government services goes that of the provisions of the welfare state, which is one of the latest marks of the developed community. Health services for mother and child, care for the aged, assistance for the destitute, all make demands both on a country's material resources, since they have to be paid for out of taxation or other levy on the national wealth, and also on its manpower.

Finally, attention must be drawn to the absence in the underdeveloped country of that legacy of capital equipment which past generations have constructed and bequeathed to all advanced societies. Railways, roads, docks and harbour facilities, electricity plants, schools and universities. All are essential, and all are found to some degree, however limited, in every country today. But the extent to which they are present is to a very considerable degree the extent of a country's economic development. They are one of the basic essentials; and they are very expensive to provide. They represent a store of wealth inherited and existing, and they are themselves wealth-generating.

There are other passages in Paul Hoffman's description which should be noted—the poverty of the countryside, the growing population, the lack of sufficiently varied exports. We shall meet and discuss all these again.

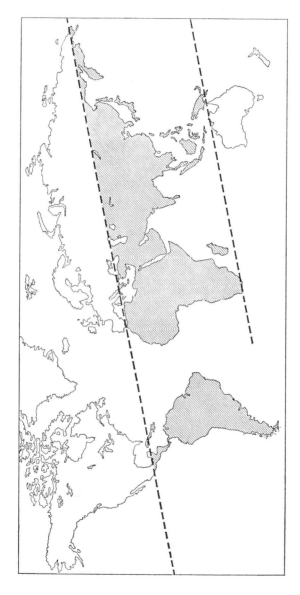

Fig. 2. The rich and poor sectors of the world.

Having briefly discussed some of the features which are recognised as typical of the poorer communities of the world, we should, before leaving the subject, consider just where these communities are to be found.

The answer is a rather surprising one. If you draw a straight line across the world east-north-east from the south-eastern tip of North America, through the Panama Canal and the Straits of Gibraltar, and across Asia to a point somewhere north of the Bering Straits, you will find that, with minor exceptions, the people in the areas to the north of the lines are enjoying a tolerable if not always completely satisfying standard of living, while those to the south are mainly poor and hungry.

To the south lie the whole of South America and Africa, and all of Asia except for part of Asiatic Russia. Above the line are North America, Europe and most of the Soviet Union. No country in this latter sector has an annual income of less than $500 per head with the exception of some Central American republics, the West Indies and the poorer southern European countries such as Greece, Yugoslavia and Spain, where the average tends to be between $300 and $500. Below the line the Union of South Africa is in some respects a very highly-developed economy, though all the wealth is not shared by all the people; Japan has recently raced towards the front and is the subject of a special section later on; and one or two of the Latin American countries have *per capita* incomes of around the $300 or $400 mark. There are also pockets of wealth here and there, often caused by the chance discovery and exploitation of oil, as in Kuwait and in parts of Venezuela. But in general the north–south division of the world is a very real one, and in the eyes of many people contains more potential dangers if left to itself than the more publicised east–west division between Communism and Western democracy.

In the continents to the south of our line live just over two-thirds of the world's population—that same two-thirds which we spoke of earlier as sharing only 15 per cent of the world's income. Within the area their conditions of life clearly vary enormously: climatic, economic, social factors differ from region to region. It is one of the inevitable limitations of a book of this length that it is not possible to treat each region as a separate problem; there will necessarily be many generalisations in the pages that follow, and therefore many statements which, while they may be generally correct, will perhaps not be accurate for every particular territory. Thus, one of India's basic problems is that of population, with over 500 million people pressing hard on the means of subsistence, and a very large rate of population increase. In Africa, however, there is no overall pressure on space, but a very big problem results from the division of Africa into a large number of often quite tiny states, most of which can never be self-supporting. The frontiers of the new African states have for the most part been drawn for no economic or geographical reason, but merely because they correspond to the old partitions created by colonial conquest; and both in their number and in their illogicality they present the African leaders with an obstacle to development.

In Latin America and the Middle East there are again different conditions and different problems to solve. Anyone who is going to spend some time in one of these countries helping in any way with their development, whether on a paid professional assignment or perhaps doing a short spell of voluntary service, should make some attempt to ascertain the peculiar conditions of that country as a prelude to visiting it.

Quantitatively as well as qualitatively there are variations between one region and another. All are poor, but some are worse off than others. Without paying too much attention to statistical figures, for reasons already given, it may be said that South-East Asia can probably show the most painful scenes of poverty in the world; the sight of beggars dying in the streets is known to many who have visited the great cities of India; and the incidence of disease and infant mortality is worse in this region than anywhere else.

Within the two-thirds of the world lying below our east–west breadline there is one large question-mark. The Communist People's Republic of China maintains an isolationism as complete as at any time in the past when the old Chinese Empire banned the foreigner from its territories; and the rest of the world, following the lead of the United States, has fostered this attitude by refusing to invite into the United Nations the representatives of that Republic, which is the effective government of the 750 million mainland Chinese.

As a consequence reliable information about conditions in China, and particularly statistical information, is very difficult to obtain. All one can say with confidence is that the vast population of China —nearly one in four of the world's inhabitants—have for long been among the poorest, subject periodically to famine, and living always on the borderline of starvation. We know also that at present a gigantic experiment to change those conditions is being carried out; but we know comparatively little about the details, or of the progress made.

China must therefore be excluded from most of the statements and views expressed in these pages. But the reader should never forget that, through the techniques of total planning which her government is using, with everything subordinated to material development, China must eventually emerge to a position of economic strength and importance, though no one can say how fast this growth will be. Already her atomic explosions have startled the world.

A distinguished American writer, Dr. Stringfellow Barr, once wrote a pamphlet called *Let's Join the Human Race*, in which he urged the necessity of a world-wide approach to the problem of the development of our human and material resources. His thesis is to a large extent the same as that which is argued out in the succeeding chapters; and the isolation of a quarter of the human race from any but the smallest contact with the rest of the world is a matter which should exercise all our minds.

Further Study

What are the real conditions of life for the ordinary citizen in some of the poorest parts of the world—is the typical Oxfam picture of a starving child fair comment on these conditions? Books and films on individual countries— on India, Vietnam, Central Africa, Haiti or other Latin American countries, can build up a picture of human life in these areas.

Statistical facts about poverty in the underdeveloped countries are easily obtainable from reference books, particularly U.N. publications. A number of the books listed after Chapters 6, 7, and 8 are also useful here.

Born to Hunger, Arthur Hopcraft (Pan Books) gives a journalist's report of poverty-stricken areas, and its accounts of work in the field can be read in conjunction with Chapter 6 and Part III generally.

PART II

Development of the Rich Countries

CHAPTER 3

The Development of the West

THE lower part of our map is poor, the upper, by any comparative standard, is wealthy. Why the difference? What is it that has been responsible for the fact that Europe, North America and certain other smaller areas no longer show those marks of poverty which we discussed in the last chapter?

Because the tremendous growth of science and technology in the last few centuries has been largely confined to what we call the Western world, it is easy for us who live there to assume that we are in fact superior beings and that it is our greater intelligence and ability that has been responsible.

One should look very carefully into history before unreservedly accepting this argument, flattering to us though it may be. Professor P. M. S. Blackett, in his presidential address to the British Association in 1957 on "Technology and World Advancement", said:

> "To the question why what happened did happen, I do not think there is an agreed answer. Certainly it had nothing to do with any inherent European superiority—indeed, the history of the previous millenia might well have suggested the opposite. Most probably it was differences in social and economic organisation which were the decisive factors."

The improvement in our mastery over the resources of the earth, in our standard of living, has not proceeded at a steady rate of increase over the whole of man's time on earth, or, indeed, over the period of recorded history. There has been an immense and rapid development in more or less recent times, and the start of this can be dated back very approximately to the sixteenth and seventeenth centuries. Obviously no precise date can be given in matters like this; you cannot say that before such and such a date living standards rose slowly or not at all, whereas after it there was a rapid rise. But the economic historians would mostly agree that before 1500 there were only slow and halting improvements, that for the next two hundred and fifty years the pace began to quicken, and that since 1750 progress has been rapid and consistent—so that in the last two hundred years man's economic wealth, in the Western world at least, has increased more than over thousands of years before.

Just as the beginning of the modern period of quick economic growth cannot be given an exact date, so there is no simple reason why it happened when it did, or where it did.

It has been pointed out that even prehistoric man made sufficient technological progress to work in most of the fields which are basic to life today. He cooked and prepared food, he built houses, he worked leather and textiles, he made weapons and used copper and bronze. But his motive force was that of human labour; machines were yet to come.

The early civilisations can show some remarkable technological achievements. The Pyramids of Egypt are only the best-known of ancient engineering feats. Professor Blackett, in the address quoted, says:

"Abundant evidence proves the high level of technological achievement at a very early date. The astonishing building feats of the Egyptians and Mesopotamians are world-famous. Less widely known are the gigantic town-planned cities of Northern India, such as Mohenjo Daro which flourished over 4,000 years ago, with their main drainage systems, vast granaries, and citizen's houses far better than those lived in by most Indians to-day. Innumerable examples abound in our museums or are illustrated in our histories, demonstrating the astonishing technical triumphs of antiquity. The stern beauty of the 4,000-year-old bronze head of Sargon the Great, or the overpowering grandeur of the 3,000-year-old inner coffin of Tutankhamen, alone suffice to prove that the highest artistry was allied to superb technical skill. The modernity in design of many articles of domestic use in ancient times is most striking. A wooden chair or a manicure set from the Egyptian New Empire of 1000 B.C. would not look out of place in the most up-to-date shop-window to-day, and might well be better made. A high level of domestic culture was by no means restricted to a few monarchs and officials.

The cities of Crete, Babylonia and Egypt around 2000 B.C. must have abounded in comfortable and cultivated people who led very pleasant lives, almost as refined and luxurious as prosperous people enjoy to-day. . . . The contribution of China to the history of technology is only now beginning to be revealed, particularly by Joseph Needham and Wang Ling in 'Science and Civilisation in China'. Far Eastern technology appears to have been supreme between 500 B.C. and A.D. 1500. Belief in Europe of the technological superiority of the Far East was indeed widespread from Marco Polo in the thirteenth century to the French missionaries of the eighteenth."

The irrigation of the early Assyrians in Mesopotamia, or the amazing mountain-cities of the Aztecs and the terraced masonry which they built to preserve their soil from being washed away are other examples. Nearer home, the roads and aqueducts of the Romans still remind us of their skill and resource.

But the basis of all these achievements was human labour. It was the existence of a slave economy, in which man was a cheap and expendable commodity, that enabled the early empires to create their monuments and public works. And, by simple economic law, if human (or animal) labour was so cheap and abundant, there was no particular incentive to look for substitutes: so much machinery as was used remained primitive and crude. "Those in authority were not interested in mechanisation except in certain fields like mining, war engines and public works. . . . Science was not yet aware of its task to assist the engineers in conquering the forces of nature for the common good" (R. J. Forbes and E. J. Dijksterhuis, *A History of Science and Technology*).

Science, in fact, was in those days regarded rather as a branch of religion or philosophy. Even the great Archimedes "held mechanical work and all practical acts as ignoble and sordid". Only indirectly was science used to help solve practical problems; and the technique of gaining knowledge by the process of careful experiment to test one's hypothesis—the whole basis of modern science—was rarely used.

Thus, up to the Middle Ages it would seem that it would have been impossible for any observer from another planet to see where the breakthrough was to come—to detect that in a century or two one small half-continent was destined to blossom forth into an age of expansion on every front which was to leave the rest of the world far behind for many generations, and was profoundly to alter the whole history of mankind. The advances were economic and political, social and cultural; and they were scientific.

We have now to examine the causes of this expansion.

It has been noted that the technical wonders of the ancient world were based on human labour, which was plentiful and cheap. If a slave died from ill-treatment, from disease or neglect, there were others to take his place. But by the time of the Middle Ages men were becoming less expendable. From slavery and serfdom Western Europe was moving to a system of paying wages for labour. There was a considerable growth of towns and of trade between town and country, and in Italy the towns became the city states which fought fiercely for their independence against the traditional feudal nobility. In these cities, and later in the cities of Germany and England, the dominant class was that of the merchants, whose prosperity depended on trade and who benefited from technical advances.

As the profitability of slavery and then serfdom became less men began to cultivate other sources of power; but while the Middle Ages lasted the water-mill and the windmill, means of harnessing natural energy, were the principal of these sources.

One achievement of the medieval world, however, was of incalculable importance, and indispensable for what followed. This was the invention of printing. The wide spread of knowledge and education which was a necessary part of the development of the Western world would have been impossible if the technical means had not been to hand.

This particular example, incidentally, illustrates how much the reasons for Western expansion were interrelated. The Chinese had invented and made considerable use of printing as far back as the eighth century, and by the time the Battle of Hastings was being fought they had developed movable type. But both the nature of the Chinese language and also the very different social conditions existing in China at the time acted as obstacles to the same sort of use being made of the technique there as in Europe.

Such trends were among those which prepared the way for the tremendous surge of energy and expansion which started around 1500 and which allows us to date the beginnings of modern history from then. Around this time other factors developed, leading finally to an irresistible force which created the empires of the eighteenth century and the factories of the nineteenth, and is still unspent today. Of these factors we may isolate five as being the most significant. To some extent they are interdependent. To some extent they grew inevitably from their past and had to wait until man and his environment were ripe for them. But it was the coming of all these together which revolutionised society in the years from the sixteenth century on. This interdependence is a factor of importance when we consider the undeveloped world today.

The five points that we isolate are:

1. The new scientific and humanistic outlook of men which followed the Renaissance.
2. The growth in education and in the opportunities for spreading information which the discovery of printing made possible.
3. The growth in the use of machinery.
4. The existence of increasingly large sums of money looking for a profitable outlet—of capital for investment, as the economist would call it.
5. The discovery of the New World which opened up new markets and new sources of raw materials for the adventuring Western Europeans from Bristol, from Lisbon, from Cadiz and Brest.

Clearly without that attitude in the minds of men which led them to take full advantage of their circumstances there would have been no scientific revolution, no industrial expansion, no major changes in society.

For a thousand years after the fall of the Roman Empire the greatest authority in Europe was the Church. During this time its contribution to the growth of European civilisation was incalculable; the doctrines of Christianity, however imperfectly realised, softened the hard brutality of life in the Dark Ages after the Goths had overrun Italy, and throughout the whole of the period up to the Renaissance it was the Church which kept some tradition of learning, of art, and of good conduct in a tough world.

But the Church was in some ways a very conservative body which resisted any challenge to its authority and to those religious truths which it regarded as divinely entrusted to it. Secular rulers challenged its power, usually with only limited success. Man fulfilled himself most completely by serving God in humility and obedience, and this life was only a preparation for the next. It ill suited a man to lay up for himself treasure in this world; the sufferings of poverty and disease which were a part of most people's existence could be borne much more patiently if they were likely to help you into paradise. All human knowledge was a part of religion. Science, as we have noted, had throughout the ancient world been regarded as an appendage of religion and philosophy, and this attitude persisted under the traditions of the Medieval Church. The treatment of Galileo, who ventured to assert the claims of scientific truth even if this conflicted with the Church's teaching, was a natural result of this general ideology.

But with the Renaissance, which set men discovering ideas and philosophies which had flourished in Greece and Rome and which showed that there were aspects of life and approaches to it quite different from the values which the Church was teaching, there came a changed attitude. There was a new spirit of enquiry, and a refusal to accept traditions without examining the reasons for them. Renaissance man found his main interest not in the supernatural, but in the nature of the physical world and in man himself. The artists of the Italian Renaissance, like Michelangelo, studied the human form and were concerned to depict its beauty and strength in natural realism; and the scientists set out to discover the secrets of nature with no purpose other than that of finding the truth.

Because there was this emphasis on things human, we can speak of this age as the age of humanism—when the idea first developed that man has the power within himself, without outside help, to mould the world into the shape that he chooses.

It has been said that Leonardo da Vinci, that greatest of all Renaissance figures, used to buy caged birds and, when he had bought them, would open the cage and let them fly away: and this action has fittingly been compared to the whole temper of the Renaissance. Man's spirit, which had been caged, was henceforth to be free to roam where it willed.

This intellectual revolution, which had to precede the material revolution, was in full spate by the fifteenth century. There were forerunners of the Renaissance even as far back as Roger Bacon in the thirteenth century, who was one of the earliest to envisage the use of experiment as a means towards the application of knowledge to practical ends—i.e. the application of science to technology. But the period around 1500 was the time when the new ideas were fully establishing themselves—the period of Da Vinci (1452–1519), Erasmus (1467–1536) and Michelangelo (1475–1564).

Although the artistic and general cultural achievements of the Renaissance spirit are among its greatest gifts to mankind, for our particular purpose we are more concerned with the change which took place in the attitude to science and to the facts of the physical world. And more particularly we should note the changed views as to the relations between science and technology which followed.

The work of Galileo, whom we have mentioned as indicative of the conflict between the medieval and the Renaissance spirits, shows the new understanding by scientists of the real nature of physical science—of the need to proceed by proven steps from one experiment and observation to another, gradually building up a tested body of facts. But from 1600 onwards there was also a vast change in the idea of the function which science should play. The Dutchman Stevin wanted to make the fruits of science accessible to all, and in this country Francis Bacon, as far back as the Elizabethan age, urged that the knowledge of the natural world obtained by science should be available to those who could apply it in technology, so that industry and trade could benefit. The seventeenth and eighteenth centuries were the period when many of the learned societies were formed, and it is worth quoting the charter of the Royal Society, in which the Society is directed to promote the "improvement of all useful arts, manufactures, mechanical practices, engines and inventions".

These two mental attitudes go far to provide the foundation for the great leap forward of the Western half of Europe after 1600. Firstly, the questing mind which seeks to explore the secrets of the universe—or, indeed, literally to explore, as this era did, the unknown parts of our own world; and, secondly, the realisation that the application of science to industry and agriculture could profoundly affect and improve conditions of life.

It was this growing link between science and technology that led to all the inventive genius of the Industrial Revolution, the steam engine of Watt, the machines which changed the whole character of the textile industries, the improvements in steel production and the rest with which our history books have made us so familiar.

It is worthy of note that most of these inventions were in fact the work not of scientists but of technicians. For example, James Hargreaves, who invented the mechanical spinning jenny in 1767, was a Blackburn weaver who wanted to provide more yarn for his weavings; Samuel Crompton, too, was a weaver, concerned to improve the quality of his thread. James Watt was a humble mathematical instrument maker and mechanic who was practically concerned with the ineffectiveness of the early steam engines of Newcomen and patented his own much more efficient engine as the first of a series of mechanical inventions which revolutionised the application of mechanical power to industry.

We see, in short, at this point the coming together of several influences. The invention of printing made the dissemination of knowledge on a vast scale a practical possibility; the surge of intellectual interest and the freeing of the mind from the restrictions of medieval religious dogmatism encouraged the full use of this medium in spreading knowledge and education; the same intellectual liveliness created the modern scientific attitude of systematic practical experiment to prove hypotheses; and the mechanics and technicians profited by both the improved education and the increased scientific knowledge to adapt and improve their machines. This latter process was greatly assisted by the learned societies organised to improve the crafts by the spread of scientific education. From all this grew the spiral of rapidly increasing productivity based on substituting ever more efficient machines for human labour.

The revolution of ideas, however, was only one part of the reason for the revolution in production. There are those who argue that all changes in man's state are caused by economic factors—by changes in the conditions under which he works and finds his means of subsistence; and although this argument, like those of so many specialists, can be carried to excess if it is used to exclude all other reasons for change, it has nevertheless a very real basis of truth.

Certainly at the time of which we are writing there was a great deal of change in the economic process.

Mention has already been made of the fact that by the beginning of the modern period in Western Europe money was in far greater use as a basis for the payment of labour and the carrying out of business transactions. Where the medieval labourer was entitled to his cottage home because of the days of labour service which he gave to his lord, many peasants were now receiving a money wage and paying rent to a landlord. In the cities the increase in trading and commerce led to the need for more frequent use of money.

Under the Catholic Church in the Middle Ages the charging of interest for lending money had been regarded as un-Christian (which had the effect of leaving all such transactions to the Jews). But with the increasing demand for money from merchants and others, and with the spread of new ideas generally, banking and money-lending became a very profitable, and in time a very respectable occupation. For many years these two operations were combined; and, indeed, even today banks have two main and not always easily reconciled functions—that of acting as a deposit for money, where a man can leave his spare cash and savings in safe custody, and even earn a little interest on them; and that of lending money.

From the earliest days of European banking the facilities for using money as a means for oiling the wheels of trade expanded quickly. Cheques, bills of exchange, and all the other mechanisms of banking were developed. When, at a later period, production units grew in size and the large factory or works became the rule rather than the exception in many industries the need for investment and capital became ever more urgent; and the financial machinery became ever more complex and varied to serve this need.

In view of the importance of investment to the whole problem of development a brief and simple explanation of the theory of investment is in place at this point.

Investment is the process of putting resources to a use which will come to fruition in the future, as opposed to the immediate consumption of resources. To spend a shilling on your bus fare to work is spending for immediate consumption; to walk to work and put the shilling into a savings fund so that you can later buy a bicycle or motor scooter is to invest the shilling. You relinquish the immediate pleasure and profit obtained by a bus ride to work in order to gain a greater profit at a future date.

This is the essential principle of investment—that you are holding something back from immediate consumption in order that you may gain a greater economic satisfaction in the future.

Investment is not the same thing as saving. You may save your shilling and keep it in an old sock under the bed; this is not investment, though you have withdrawn it from current spending. You may indeed save it and spend it on bus fares next month rather than this, because the weather is likely to be less attractive for walking next month, or because your time will be more at a premium then. But the essence of investment is that the money not spent is instead put to some use by which it fructifies and creates greater wealth, so that the reward of the immediate deprivation of consuming power is an increase in satisfaction later.

One of the most common examples of investment in business is the use of machinery. This introduces the concept of capital goods as opposed to consumer goods. You can wear a suit, which is therefore a consumer good, even though it does not wear out, i.e. is not "consumed", immediately; and a tailor can make you a suit by hand. But he is more likely to use machinery. You cannot wear the machinery, but its use will enable the tailor to make more suits; someone in the past, by producing the suit-making machinery, has made it possible for more suits to be produced. The machinery is a capital good.

Most machinery is designed in order eventually to lead to the production of more consumer goods; the machinery itself usually has no direct value in satisfying consumers' needs, but has value in that it indirectly creates goods which satisfy those needs; and the reason why it exists is because it will produce those goods more rapidly and cheaply than can be done without it. Thus, a mine-owner may set men to work excavating the earth and hewing coal by hand, and the miners will be directly producing the end-product, the consumer good of coal. But if the mine-owner, instead of engaging men to hew coal by hand, engages men to construct mining machinery and then installs this and employs others to operate it, the ultimate production of coal will be infinitely greater. The owner will have had to defer any immediate gain, and will have had to invest considerable sums of money before he gets any return for his expenditure; but in the future, in the long run, he, and the community, will be immeasurably better off.

(Incidentally, though coal is referred to above as a consumer good, it is of course one of those commodities which can be either. If you buy coal and destroy it at once by burning it in your grate for heating your room you have used it as a consumer good; but when it is used, for example, in a steel mill to create the heat needed for the furnaces which will produce steel castings or railway engines then it is functioning as a part of capital goods. The distinction is not always very easy to draw, but the principle is clear enough.)

This conception of investment must be seen to apply to every form of withdrawal of resources from immediate production of consumer goods. Thus, education and training are a very important form of investment, since, in their vocational sense at least, they are designed to make a person a more productive worker in the future at the cost of taking him away from immediate productive work in the present. A boy of eleven or twelve could be occupied in a factory on some unskilled occupation, but we consider it much more worth while to everyone that he should be educated and trained far beyond that age so that he can eventually be a much more useful member of the community.

The importance of investment to the economic development of a country must now be evident. And it should also be evident that the more primitive a community the harder it is to invest. In a state where everyone is working on the soil with primitive implements and methods, and a family can barely wrest a subsistence for its own members through unceasing labour, there are no spare resources. Everything is spent on the day-by-day harrowing task of producing enough to keep starvation at bay.

Not until, by some process, some resources can be set aside from the daily struggle and can be put to investment can this situation be eased. If one family can be enabled to grow enough food for two, then the labour and skill of the second family can begin to be used in plans for the future—the men can build machines, the boys can go to school and be trained for more productive tasks when they are older.

What is more, once this process of investing spare resources for future good has begun, every step forward makes the next progressively easier. At first such resources are few in proportion to the whole wealth of the community, but as the bringing into use of machinery and of wiser and better trained minds and bodies has its effect, that available proportion gets greater. The first step is the most difficult.

We shall come to see this as in many ways the fundamental problem of development. It is the problem of what is called "take-off" —the change from a primitive and mainly agricultural condition to the first stages of industrialisation, of capitalism, using that word not in its political sense, but as a description of the economic state where production is mainly carried out by enterprises which (whether state- or private-controlled) have a considerable expenditure on capital goods in their structure.

(It is estimated that for heavy industries such as steel the amount of capital employed is between £5000 and £10,000 per man employed; and the whole trend of modern automated industry is towards a still heavier ratio of investment. Compare this with the completely non-capitalised condition of the peasant communities in most Asian and African countries.)

We shall now return to our survey of Western European development and see more clearly the role which investment played. Reference has already been made to the increasing use of money towards the end of the Middle Ages. Now, one of the principal characteristics and advantages of money is the ease with which it can be transferred from one use to another. If your wealth is in land or in durable goods you may be very rich, but these things are only capable of certain limited uses; you can grow things on land or build houses on it, but you may not want to do either of these things. Money, however, can serve as a means whereby you can transfer the wealth inherent in the land or goods you own to other purposes.

As money began to be used more in Western Europe men of substance, whether landlords or merchants, began to accumulate wealth in that particular form. It is said that on the Continent this surplus wealth—surplus in the sense that it was not needed for immediate consumption—arose mainly in the form of rents accruing to landlords, whereas in England capital came from trade rather than from rents. In particular, a large number of the rising middle class made fortunes from the export of wool and other commodities to Europe; and the richest men in England in Elizabethan times were indeed very rich, able to afford a quite luxurious existence.

The changing attitude to usury and interest which we have already mentioned was of great significant at this point. The Medieval Church said that it was wrong for a Christian to make money by charging interest on a loan; but by the sixteenth century there were on the one hand many more people who could see a possible means of creating wealth for themselves and others if only they could borrow some capital; and, on the other hand, many more who had the money to lend. It was inevitable that the two groups should come together, and under the pressure of economic forces and the weakening of the Catholic Church's authority it became accepted that a man who lent money was performing a service to the borrower, and was therefore entitled to charge interest on his loan.

The outlook of the Puritans was highly favourable to the new forces of capital, and Calvin gave a moral sanction to worldly success.

The ease of transfer of money from one use to another was now fully utilised, and the financing of new productive enterprises made easy.

Another very great spur to economic growth at this time was the discovery of the New World and the route to the Indies. Historically, the first consequence of this was the introduction to the West of many new commodities which were brought back by the returning travellers. In particular, large quantities of gold and silver were imported to Europe and were used for adding to the existing coinage. This greatly increased the stock of money in circulation, and as a result of this prices rose by leaps and bounds. In England food prices doubled between 1540 and 1640; in Italy prices as a whole doubled in the sixteenth century. In Spain, where the imports of the precious metals were greatest, the rising costs were even more prodigious, and in fifty years from 1560 Spanish prices trebled.

Now, although inflation, and particularly uncontrolled inflation, has many unpleasant effects, there is no doubt that, in certain situations, the increased availability and circulation of money can help economic expansion. The quick profits which can be obtained when prices of goods are rising can stimulate business enterprise and investment; and there is much evidence that the price rises of the sixteenth century did just this. Wages of labourers lagged far behind prices and therefore profits increased; and the wealth thus accumulated provided more capital for further profitable investment.

Meanwhile, other effects of the new discoveries beyond the seas were increased imports of goods which could satisfy the growing demands of the population—spices, carpets, tobacco, cottons; and conversely new markets opened overseas for European exports of manufactures. This was the age of the great sailing ships, with all their romance and adventure, their squalor and danger. Thrilling voyages of exploration were accompanied by cruel disciplines and privations endured for the chance of great wealth. The profitability of trade with the inhabitants of the new countries was enormous, and much impetus was given to the formation of chartered companies of merchants to exploit the new opportunities. The period of the East India Company, the Hudson Bay Company and others was at hand; and since the setting up of these companies and the equipping of ships for the long voyages required much capital, the technique of the joint stock company, which enables men to pool their savings in a business organisation, was evolved, and a further step taken towards creating capacity for profitable investment.

At this stage of development the British economy benefited considerably by the influx of capital from abroad. The Dutch in particular invested heavily in England during the sixteenth and seventeenth centuries, and the East India Company was one of the enterprises which was partly dependent on Dutch capital.

As time went on the importance of the overseas trade grew greater, and by the eighteenth century the establishment of trading stations and colonies had proceeded far. The eventual victory of the British in the struggle for empire was one contributory factor to the industrial supremacy of this country in the years to come. You could invest your capital in a colonial territory; you could use the armed forces of your country to protect your trade and to enable you to dictate conditions of employment and exact concessions from native rulers; and you could become wealthy either by selling cheap English goods to the native inhabitants or by establishing industry in the colonies and exploiting their raw materials. All this went to swell the revenues of the home country, and increased that surplus which could be added to the total of savings capital for investment. And, let us repeat, every investment of money in a growing economy is an assurance of future increases to the wealth-producing capacity of the country. Once economic development is under way, there is a self-perpetuating spiral of advance.

The extent to which Britain's path to wealth was smoothed by the imperial connections gives some justification to the claim that we rode to success "on the backs of the coolies". The United Kingdom's more recent colonial policy and more enlightened approach to relations with the new independent African and Asian states of the Commonwealth has done something to balance this, but, if one of the most vital requisites of development is investment, it cannot be gainsaid that we, in common with and to a greater extent than other European countries, exploited the colonial peoples. We developed some of their raw materials, their rubber, cocoa and copper; in the process of doing this we gave order and internal security; but virtually the whole surplus from the local industries, the whole profit on the trading was for re-investment at the hands and wills of British owners and British shareholders, and most of it returned to this country to speed our own prosperity rather than being retained in the country of origin.

How far did this economic domination depend on political power? After the American colonies became independent we continued to lend them capital on which we received valuable dividends, and we continued to export to them manufactured goods. The Latin American countries, in none of which had we ever held any political empire, were among our most profitable markets; we established companies there, we built their railways. Our trading prosperity in Victorian times depended not only on those areas of the map of the world which were coloured red, but equally on the variegated tints which marked the independent powers. Nevertheless, a great deal of our prosperity arose from the favourable opportunities for foreign investment and markets of all kinds, both in our own colonies and in independent but undeveloped states, with the bulk of the eventual surplus or profit coming back to England, on the grounds which no one disputed at the time, and many would not dispute now, that it was English capital, enterprise and technical skill that had developed the resources and created the new wealth.

Figures and statistics about the economy before 1800 are very difficult to come by and of doubtful value; but there is no doubt that by the eighteenth century Britain was already getting a handsome reward for her overseas activities, while at the same time industry and trade at home were now becoming profitable enough for there to be an adequate surplus for maintaining the development process out of the proceeds of industry itself. This was made much easier by the fact that the absence of any kind of workers' organisation in those days kept the wage levels persistently below those which would today be considered a fair proportion of remuneration for labour.

Perhaps this is the point at which to say a very brief word about the position of agriculture. In most writings or discussions on the revolution of productivity in Britain most emphasis is given to the industrial scene, since it is here that the achievements have been most spectacular. But the application of technology to agriculture has been of equal scope and certainly of equal importance. Indeed, it was an agricultural revolution which first speeded economic growth, when the medieval manor gave way to farming for profit and to sheep-rearing for wool; and this was matched by another similar revolution—this time more specifically a technological one —in the eighteenth century which, by reducing the numbers employed on the land, went far to provide the factory fodder for the cotton mills and the coal mines.

It was the industrialisation of Britain that made us for a time the wealthiest people in the world, and it is that industrialisation which the developing countries today see as their model; but before it was possible men had to get more food from the land.

This was done, and done most successfully in the eighteenth century. Later, when the industrial revolution was in full flood, and Britain was neglecting its farms for its factories, we were greatly helped by the opening up of the New World and the vast expansion of wheat, meat and dairy produce on the ranches and prairies of the Americas. The "workshop of the world", with a rapidly increasing population, imported cheap food in large quantities in return for its industrial products; this was a further considerable fillip to our development, and was in some respects a unique contribution to British industrial supremacy which certainly can never be repeated in the development story of any other country. It enabled us to forget the importance of agriculture in the economy as a whole— to forget that though you can exist without steel and railways and atomic power at a pinch, you cannot exist without food.

By the end of the eighteenth century everything was ready for the big leap forward. The years from 1780 to 1800 are reliably regarded as the period of "take-off" in the British economy. The new inventions were beginning to take effect and the capital was available for their exploitation. The labour force for industry was there, many of them dispossessed small farmers and unemployed agricultural labourers. The coal and iron which were the most essential commodities at this stage were available together in large quantity, and Britain also had an efficient banking system, an individualistic approach to enterprise and an overseas empire.

During the generation or two after the famous inventions of Arkwright, Watt and the others English industry grew at a hitherto unprecedented rate. There were hardly any competitors in the field, and in the absence of even the beginnings of a welfare state the capitalist owners could cash in on the profitability of the new methods without the restrictions imposed by factory inspection or wage agreements. For a hundred years before 1780 the national income had risen by little more than $\frac{1}{2}$ per cent per annum; in the next hundred years it was to increase ten or twelvefold. Industrial production doubled between 1800 and 1825 and again before 1850; by 1870 it had doubled yet again.

The detailed story of this period of Britain's expansion is so familiar that it need not occupy much space here. The first half of the nineteenth century was mainly concerned with the building-up of our basic industries; it was also the period of the transport revolution. Steamships were developed and the railway boom made many fortunes for enterprising businessmen. In 1818 it took thirty hours to go by express coach from London to York, in 1855 it took four hours by train. After 1850 the importance of science in the development of industry grew ever more apparent. Electricity came into its own, and with the invention of the telegraph and the submarine cable—the first Atlantic cable was completed in 1866—the modern era of communications began. Henceforth, however slow we may be to realise it, the world was one, since any event which happened no matter where, in New York, in Calcutta, in Moscow, was known in London almost as soon as it happened. Chemistry became an ever more important branch of industry, and with the coming of the motor-car the modern age may be said to have begun.

At the same time, people began to accept action by the state to limit the evils of unfettered private enterprise. More effective factory acts, education services, the beginnings of the welfare state and the long-delayed growth of trade unions are all seen.

Increasing competition to Britain from other countries, notably the U.S.A. and Germany, showed itself well before 1900. We know only too well today that the supremacy of the Victorian days has gone; our European rivals have caught us up and the vast productivity of the U.S.A. has outstripped us. Our reliance on the staple heavy industries which made us rich can no longer be complete, our ability eternally to import cheap food is threatened. Yet Britain remains a leading industrial power; her technological skill is still great. Her main need now is to adjust herself to the conditions of a different world from that in which her early supremacy was gained. This is another story, yet one which is not unconnected with that of the new developing powers; for in the twentieth century all our destinies are linked together. One need only mention two points which we would be most unwise to neglect. Firstly, the growth of incomes elsewhere which development will bring is the surest hope of continued markets for our best products. And secondly, a country dependent like ours on cheap food imports must view with great alarm the vast growth of the world's population and the consequent demand on food supplies unless these latter are abundantly increased to meet the greater need.

To conclude this chapter, let us summarise the stages of Western European and British industrial growth. The beginnings may be seen in the slow growth of the trading class in the free cities of the Middle Ages, in the spread of knowledge through printing, and in the coming of the Renaissance. Over a period of more than two hundred years the combined effect of scientific knowledge and technical advance, of profitable investment and individual initiative to improve oneself and of overseas expansion led to a steady growth in national wealth which eventually became the revolution in production which has created the affluent society of today. The five factors which we mentioned on page 27 are seen to be the linked threads, which, like those of Samuel Crompton's spinning mule, have led us to prosperity.

It will be seen that the problems of a country or continent which has passed through the early stages of economic development are entirely different from those of a community which has yet to reach the take-off stage. In general the latter society is static, and the problem is to prepare for change, to adapt one's habits of life and institutions to change and to overcome the inertia which comes from living mainly from day to day, unable to think of or save for the future. But the issues which concern the industrialised and developed community are the issues which arise from change; the constant adjustment to new conditions, new advances and discoveries in science, new applications of knowledge to industry, new working conditions and new skills to be attained by workers. Britain and Western Europe have long passed from the first stage; our problems today are those of adapting to change which presses on us, as it were, automatically.

Further Study

A study of any one aspect of development in the United Kingdom will show how the speed of development steadily increases once the start is assured. Transport, banking, technology, education, are all suitable subjects for such study. The growth of such institutions as parliament and central government itself, trades unions and industrial firms is also very relevant.

A History of Science and Technology by R. J. Forbes and E. J. Dijksterhuis (Penguin) usefully describes the growth of the use of tools and machines. Ritchie Calder's *The Inheritors* (Heinemann) is a fascinating account of the contribution of different civilisations.

For detailed economic histories use *Economic History of Europe*, S. B. Clough and D. W. Cole (D. C. Heath & Co.), and *Economic History of England*, M. Briggs and P. Jordan (University Tutorial Press), and for easier general reading *Britain Yesterday and To-Day*, Walter M. Stern (Longmans).

On special topics the following are useful:

The Common People, 1740–1938, G. D. H. Cole and R. Postgate (Methuen).

A History of British Trade Unionism, H. Pelling (Penguin).

The Industrial Revolution, T. S. Ashton (O.U.P.).

A History of Money, E. V. Morgan (Pelican).

CHAPTER 4

Development in Other Countries

OVER a hundred years ago the British businessman, whether banker, mill-owner or railway magnate, looked out on the world and gloried in his superiority—were not the British the workshop of the world, the most advanced and richest of peoples? But today he can see at least three other countries, quite apart from the rest of Western Europe, which have passed through the same stages from primitive conditions to modern industrialisation—the United States, the Soviet Union and Japan. It may now be useful to look at the different circumstances which accompanied the growth of each of these great communities.

I. The United States

The United States stands now as the most fully developed economically of all countries; and this despite the existence of quite considerable pockets of poverty which have been described by Gunnar Myrdal in *Challenge to Affluence*. The average income per head in U.S.A. amounts to over $3000 a year; no other country comes near this figure, Canada, with about $2150, being a rather poor runner-up. Yet before the colonisation of America a native Indian community estimated at round about a million were unable to eke out more than a bare subsistence; and before Independence in 1776 there were only about two million colonists inhabiting the East Coast area, with Indian tribes in the rest of the country. When Britain's labourers had already begun to crowd into the factories and mines the thirteen colonies were still mainly concerned with either agricultural settlement east of the Alleghanies or with pioneering into the land of the Indians through and beyond the mountains.

The story of American development may be divided into three main sections. The first lasts from the time of Independence nearly up to the Civil War. The new United States, still mainly a pastoral economy, was well behind the former mother country in industrialisation, and had indeed been deliberately kept back by the English governments. In this first period agriculture remained the most important part of the economy. The bulk of manufacturing was still carried on in the home or small shop, and such larger-scale industry as was established during this time was to a larger extent financed from Europe, and especially from the United Kingdom. This was particularly so from 1830 onwards; we can see that first of all Europe had to recover from the Napoleonic wars, and then in Britain our own industrialisation had to proceed to a stage where it no longer needed to absorb all the available native capital, and men began to look beyond their own front doors for opportunities for investment. When this time came it coincided with the growing tempo of expansion of white America westward, and many American businesses and industrial concerns of this date were financed with British capital. Even the great Pacific railways, those tremendous undertakings which have become the basis of so much legend and folklore much of which is well known to us over here, originally owed much to our money. In 1843 America owed 225 million dollars to foreign countries; in 1857 this total had risen to 375 million.

The exact period at which the American take-off occurred is a matter for some conjecture. The decade of the 1840's is a period accepted by many experts, though some would put it rather earlier. As with Britain, there was a slow build-up of forces preparatory to and paving the way for the real economic surge, which was certainly well under way by 1850.

The next period marks the conversion of the States from a predominantly agricultural economy to a major industrial power—though, because of the vast spaces of his country, the average American is able to enjoy a varied and adequate diet out of home products, and has never had, like ourselves, to depend on foreign food paid for by his own manufactures. Despite the degree of industrialisation which has been reached, United States agriculture not only still provides enough for the home population, but has very large surpluses of which to dispose.

A great deal of the capital which lay behind this second-stage expansion still came from Europe; but the Americans were increasingly becoming able to finance their own growth. In 1874 U.S.A. for the first time had an excess of exports over imports.

This perhaps more than any other was the time of the great American ideal of the independent pioneer who by his brains and initiative could become a millionaire. The lure of the frontier was still the great inspiration, and the mood of continued expansion was everywhere.

The first continental railroad was completed in 1869; gold and silver strikes were attracting thousands to the Far West. With the growth of refrigeration cattle ranching became one of the great western industries, and grain too was widely cultivated. The expanding frontier was one of the greatest of America's economic assets at this time, performing for her development much of the role that was carried out for Britain by her overseas empire. It created new sources of raw materials, new areas of agricultural land, new centres of settlement for the growing population, with all that this meant in increased demand for goods and services of all kinds. Throughout the century, and right up till the admission of Arizona and New Mexico in 1912, states were being added to the Union.

In this period, too, immigration from the Old World reached its peak. This was an almost unique feature in the American growth picture: to ever-expanding lands and opportunities westward and to ever-increasing capital, home or foreign made, was added the flood of energetic, resourceful families pouring in from every part of Europe—from Ireland, from Italy, from Germany, Poland and Russia. The Statue of Liberty beckoned them to this new world where they would build a new future for themselves; and just as their industry helped to build the wealth of their adopted country, so did their numbers add to the growing consumer market which encouraged yet more production.

Nowhere else in the world has there been to the same extent this constant vitalising influence of new labour and of new blood in a more than usually literal sense. The population of U.S.A. rose from 13 million in 1830 to 31 million in 1860 and 63 million in 1890. In the year 1850 alone, 370,000 immigrants settled in the States, and between 1860 and 1880 there was an influx of 5 million. The flood continued up to and beyond the end of the century, and by 1910 the population was 92 million.

Eventually, in the twentieth century America finally established herself in the position which she now holds—that of the leading industrial nation, with a higher productivity and higher standard of living than any other. This leadership of wealth is so fully recognised today that it is hard to realise that it is really a very new thing; and harder still in the days of American loans to Europe and massive American expenditure on the defence of the Western world as a whole to realise that in the lifetime of many who are still alive today American businessmen were owing us money, and interest income from investments across the Atlantic played a large part in balancing Britain's payments.

This last phase of American development is to date the farthest that men have yet taken the story of technical and economic advance. In it the "affluent society" can be seen coming into being, solving many of the problems of poverty and scarcity, but creating its own very different ones. In the early years of the century the increasing development of mass production methods in the factory led to very large increases in productivity. The legendary career of Henry Ford illustrates this period well. The real pioneer now was the business tycoon, who saw the possibilities of the large consumers' market and who created his business on the basic principle of producing a standardised article which modern methods of salesmanship and distribution would sell at cheap prices to millions. The Ford Model T and the Hoover are the archetypes of this era.

The two World Wars gave America an artificial advantage over Europe because of the position which she held as main provider of materials, munitions and food. This hastened her productive growth, but her industrial supremacy was already assured by 1914. Nowhere else did there exist a domestic market so large, so suitable for exploitation by mass production.

The economy created by the continuing growth of big business and of the financial mechanisms which helped to provide the capital which was required in ever-increasing quantity proved to be a complex organism which did not always work as smoothly as it was supposed to do. The recurrent slumps which put millions out of work and reached a climax in the great depression of the 1930's were the reverse side of the picture of otherwise ever-growing prosperity. These periods when the great machine of modern industry seemed temporarily to break down showed that there was yet much to learn about the effective control of this machine, particularly in its economic workings—lessons the full employment world of the 1960's claims to have learnt at least in part. At the time they caused great misery and hardship to many; yet they only slowed down and did not halt the general advance, which always picked up again with an increasing tempo after each depression.

This onward march of American production was still basically the result of a free enterprise system, of the American ideal of the "young man makes good" order. And this was so even though one should not minimise the effects of government intervention—the enormous munitions contracts and other government orders which gave an artificial boom to industry during each war, and the imaginative "New Deal" programme of Roosevelt which set the wheels turning again in the 1930's after the worst of slumps. The faults of this period, too, were the faults of the private enterprise system. Those who failed in the competitive struggle and went to the wall received little sympathy or, what is more important, help. Many fortunes were made not by giving the public goods or services which it required, but by defrauding the public or by speculation. Community services like education and hospitals were grossly inadequate by the standards of wealth which the country had won for itself in other spheres.

Yet overall the tremendous productive advances overshadowed

all failures and shortcomings. And they have today gone so far as to bring America into yet a new era—the era of automation and the computer.

Like all others, it brings its own problems. Galbraith's *The Affluent Society* gives a graphic description of some of these, with its picture of a society obsessed with its capacity for production and absorbed in the creation of markets for that production, to the extent of persuading people that they need to buy something which they really don't need at all, simply in order that it should be sold and the producers kept busy and the profits high. To ensure continuing sales some firms even produce goods which need replacement after a year or two when they are technically fully capable of making an article which will last indefinitely.

With these very real problems of the computer age we are not here concerned—the need for much vaster investment in the communal sector of education and scientific research, and the balance between science and the rest of human activity and between work and leisure. But we are concerned here to see how this fantastic development of one part of the human race links with and contrasts with the poverty and apparent failure to develop of over half of humanity whom we considered in the second chapter of this book. And the story of American development underlines again that the first step is the hardest. Once labour-saving machinery and technical advance have begun, each step forward releases new resources for yet further advance; and in America today the productivity of some industries is potentially so great that in order to keep themselves in business they have to create an artificial demand for their goods. Yet this takes place in a world where many are starving.

The foregoing brief sketch of American development should have been sufficient to show that the country's prodigious growth owed a great deal to a number of unusually favourable circumstances. There was the fact of a mother country and a parent continent which supplied the new nation with large sums of capital which put it on its feet. There were the wide open spaces which called to the pioneering spirit to push out and adventure and expand. There was the massive immigration which provided fresh labour and fresh markets to balance the growing productivity. And, finally, to enable the last leap forward which established America as the pre-eminent industrial country of the world, came the two World Wars, in which the States were the arsenal and provider-in-chief of the whole Allied world.

Such a fortunate series of circumstances is unlikely ever to be repeated; and, although the main credit goes to the industry and initiative of those multitudes of American citizens, whether first, second or third generation Americans, whose work created this wealth, the favourable conditions must be appreciated. Because, though this wealth was not created without hardship, suffering and a great deal of exploitation and inhumanity, yet it was created within the framework of a free democratic society. And this itself is a notable feature of the American story. It will be seen that other countries, and notably the Soviet Union, which we next consider, have not had so many advantages; and it may not always be so easy to maintain fundamental freedoms when conditions are consistently adverse. This is a problem which the developing countries have to face; and the lesson of the great American story of growth is lost if it is not realised that different circumstances may call for different solutions. It is certainly fair to assume that if conditions had been less favourable, then either the American achievement would not have been so complete and rapid, or it would have been accomplished at the expense of some of that private individual freedom and democracy which the Americans treasure and which is a proud feature of their society.

II. The Soviet Union

The economic rise of the Soviet Union is a more recent story, and one on which a great deal of emotional feeling sometimes gathers. The economic facts, however, are fairly clear, and they have important lessons for us. The student must of course try to distinguish between these facts and the judgments of value which are made about the Soviet system as a whole.

It would be a mistake to think that nothing was done to begin to develop Russia before the Revolution. Under the Czars Russia alternated between periods of looking westwards and emulating European ways and periods of relapse into autocratic isolation.

By 1914 there were pockets of considerable industrial development in the Don Basin, in Poland (then a Russian province) and round Moscow. And most of such industry as existed was reasonably advanced, since its equipment and factories were new.

But the country as a whole was a vast agricultural area; and the agriculture was by no means productive and up-to-date. Only one in ten of the population lived by industry; and even of these many were only part-time factory workers, who also spent some of their time working on the land. Clearly these were not conditions likely to lead to swift development, with so much over-employment in the agricultural sector.

The condition of the peasants was in many ways not far removed from that which obtains in many of the developing countries today, although there were many different levels of prosperity or lack of it. An official investigation in 1895 reported that in 46 provinces of European Russia more than a half of the peasantry lacked the "19 poods of breadstuffs necessary for the needs of a peasant household".

The low productivity of agriculture compared with other European countries was the main reason for the low standard of life of the people. To make matters worse, most of the existing industry was foreign-owned and financed. Britain, France and America had all invested quite considerable sums in Russian industry, and to pay for both the loans and the interest on the Western capital a hungry, ill-fed Russia exported considerable quantities of grain—thus providing a further analogy with many of the present-day developing countries who export raw materials and whose industry is, or at least was until recently, owned by foreigners, usually European.

The Communist leaders came to power after the Revolution with a considerable knowledge of the ways in which Western countries had industrialised, and a determination to plan the whole resources and life of Russia in the direction of economic development. But circumstances could hardly have been worse. For four years they were faced with the aftermath of war and revolution and then with a war against the White Russians and their allies from outside which consumed a vast quantity of resources which should have been helping to build up the peacetime industry, and which left chaos and destruction over large areas of the country. The anti-revolutionary forces aided by the allies invaded and occupied large areas of the land. During the first four years of the régime, therefore, the Soviet leaders had to impose a war economy.

By 1921 the country was in ruins. The Bolsheviks were beginning to build up a machine of state control, but the productive life of the country was almost at a standstill. Industrial output was less than a fifth of pre-war, and the area of cultivated land was half what it had been in 1914. The monetary process had broken down and the rouble was valueless. In the countryside the revolutionary leaders had broken up all the larger estates and given the land to the peasants; but these estates had been the most productive farms, and the small farms now owned by the people could do little more than provide a bare living for those who worked on them. Moreover, the peasants were revolting against the Government's plans to take their crops from them, with promises to give them in return manufactured goods which the factories were barely able to produce.

At this point Lenin introduced the New Economic Policy, which temporarily re-established the rights of private trading and cultivation. He also appealed to the outside world to help by providing capital for industry. But the Communist régime had already confiscated the investments and enterprises which had been established by foreigners under the Czars; and this, added to the general hostility of capitalists and governments outside Russia to the new rulers, meant that there was no hope at all of calling on foreign loans and funds to help investment. The Russians had to go it alone.

The Soviet leaders started therefore in the most difficult of circumstances. On the other hand, they did have the advantage of having been able to study the economic causes and progress of Western development, and they could benefit from the acquired technical knowledge of the twentieth century. Thus, when the British industrial revolution began, the use of electricity was unknown, transport was in a most primitive state and railways and steamships did not exist; the modern chemical industry and the internal combustion engine still lay in the future. But the Russians could at least inherit the know-how which resulted from the hundred and fifty years of European and American technological progress. They were able also to plan with a realisation of the importance of heavy industries, and with some idea of the economic processes necessary for rapid development. They were able thereby to make much more speedy progress once their plans did begin to bear fruit.

Conditions still remained desperately difficult, but throughout the 1920's there was a steady improvement, both on the land and in the factories. Under the less confiscatory measures of the N.E.P. the peasants began to produce more food. In industry the output of pig iron in 1919 had been a derisory 4 per cent of the 1913 level; but by the time of the first Five-Year Plan in 1928 the pre-war output had been almost equalled.

The rate of development, however, was much too slow. The introduction of the first Five-Year Plan was the signal that the Russian rulers were determined to force the pace and to use every means at the disposal of total government to do so. Belts already tight were to be pulled in still further.

The plan gave the highest priority to massive capital investment in heavy industry. To provide the labour force required many workers were directed from the farms to the factories. But a much harder task was to provide the vast sums of capital in a country which was still poor and which could not call on foreign funds. The only course, if heavy industry was to be satisfied, was to cut down the consumption of the people to an absolute minimum, and to force from them savings which would go into industry. To feed the industrial population the Government confiscated food from the farms. In a time when men and women were near starvation the Government even exported food in order to buy machinery and technical aid from abroad, thus repeating the policies which had obtained before the revolution. The people were squeezed tight; strict rationing was imposed.

The policy of developing heavy industry worked, but at a cost.

In order to be able to plan the whole economy and not only the industrial sector of it the Five-Year Plan envisaged a change in agricultural policy, based on widespread collectivisation and the withdrawal of most of the concessions to the private enterprise of peasants made by the N.E.P. By 1931 over half the farmers were in the collective kolkhozes, but the price was terrible. Many of the peasants, particularly the richer kulaks, rebelled against the policy. Farm output dropped to a fraction of what it had been in 1928, and there was widespread famine before the end of the first Plan. In 1933 there were less than one half the livestock on Soviet farms that there had been in 1928, and this loss was not recouped until twenty years later. There was wholesale repression, and mass deportation of the more recalcitrant peasants.

To ease matters the Government built up model farms and embarked on a process of mechanisation, setting up machine-tractor stations from which the farmers could borrow; but these projects needed time before they could make much impact.

Quite apart from the intense human suffering which took place at this time, did the Soviet rulers misjudge their agricultural policy? They were right in saying that heavy industry must develop faster; they were quite right to try to increase the proportion of industrial workers at the expense of agriculture; and they had learnt the economic lesson that this can only be done if agricultural productivity can be raised, so that more food is grown by fewer people.

Their mistake was in thinking that collectivisation would do this. Even here they may theoretically have been right, since the whole trend of modern agriculture is towards larger and more scientifically managed units. But they misjudged the extent to which a dissatisfied peasantry can be driven; and in so doing they exposed one of the weaknesses from which a totalitarian government suffers. In a democracy the degree of opposition to the proposed collectivisation would have shown itself so strongly that a prudent government would have altered the plan; the Soviet system at that time allowed no such opportunity for dissent to be expressed, with the result that the leaders could not be aware of the potential dangers to this aspect of their planning.

Yet the first Five-Year Plan achieved results in the industrial field which were truly remarkable; and by the end of the second Plan, in 1938, the Soviet Union had gone a very long way towards becoming a major industrial power. The figures in Table 1 give an indication of the progress achieved.

TABLE 1.

	1913	1928 (beginning of first 5-Year Plan)	1938	1948	1961
Steel (million tons)	4·2	4·3	18	19	70
Grain ,, ,,	80	73	95	115	137
Coal ,, ,,	29·1	35·5	133	150	377
Electricity (1,000 million kilowatt hours)	2	5	39	66	327

The third Plan was launched in 1938, but the Second World War prevented its full implementation.

Despite the setback caused by the terrible devastation of that war, the upward movement of Soviet production has, as everyone is aware, gone ahead at ever faster rates since 1945. The Russian achievements in science and space research have shown the rest of the world that in technical and scientific development at least the Soviet Union has done much to overhaul the West; and this fact is obviously of great significance to people of the emerging countries, existing as they do in a poverty as great as or greater than that of the Russian peasantry before the 1914 War.

The gross output of the Soviet Union has mushroomed and is now several times what it was before the Second World War. The economic planning of the régime is still carried out on rigid state-controlled lines, but, with the essential industries now well established and research and training as advanced as anywhere in the world, there are signs that the basic problem of economics, which is to decide on the allocation of resources between one end and another, may be increasingly shared by the people, and that Comrade Ivan may be able to a greater extent to influence what the country produces by the power of his purse. Probably only the cold war has prevented this process from going further as yet.

It is impossible to make very accurate comparisons of Soviet standards with those of capitalist countries, because the criteria of measurement are in some respects quite different. But if the figure of income of $900 per head per year, which is a rough estimate based on 1963 figures, may seem as yet very much behind Western levels, it must be appreciated that this is a 100 per cent increase since 1954, as compared with about a 50 per cent increase in the West.

Can we disentangle from the Soviet story some lessons for the future?

Firstly, let it be clear that though the Soviet received no loans or other financial help from the outside world for many years, they were able to make quite considerable use of the technical skill and knowledge of foreign experts. In the inter-war years British, American and German engineers were advising the Russian leaders, and the part which has been played by German scientists—not all of them entirely free agents, no doubt—since the 1939–45 war in establishing Russia's leading place in the space race is claimed by some to be very large.

But although such technical aid enabled the Soviet Union to make use of the more advanced knowledge of the Western nations, it did not help with the basic problem of discovering spare resources through the investment of which capital development could proceed and the knowledge acquired could be fully utilised. Now it may not be very difficult or painful to put by one-tenth or more of your income for saving or future investment when you are already comfortably off; but it is a very different thing to have to save when you are short of the necessities of life.

The Russian leaders in the 1920's knew full well the necessity of investment on a large scale. They regarded it as social investment, by and on behalf of the community as a whole. They were not concerned with the question of investment as an individual matter, and saw no reason why the individual should be paid interest for the loan of his money. In any case, it was clear that any attempt to finance development in Russia through money loans from individuals would have a derisory result because of the poverty of the people. Private business could certainly not have raised from within Russia the large sums needed for modern industry under conditions of free enterprise. High rates of interest have to be paid in an undeveloped country if they are to attract the limited amount of capital which is available; and in the process the lenders will achieve a status out of all proportion to their value to the community. Even if foreign capital had been available too much reliance on it could have meant mortgaging the future in repayments and probably accepting restrictions on socialist experiment and an economically "colonial" status.

To avoid this the Communists went behind the money façade of investment as it generally appears to Western eyes, brought up as we are on a money economy, to the reality of investment. This reality is to be found in the use which is made of real resources, such as men, land and materials. The extent to which these real resources are used to create wealth in the future rather than immediate consumer goods like food and clothing is, as we have seen, the true measure of investment.

In a free enterprise economy like the British and American these things may be calculated in terms of money. This is because the normal method of attracting resources into any form of activity is to bid for them by an offer of money. But in a system where the state plans everything centrally, and is indeed prepared to adopt measures of compulsion rather than persuasion if necessary, it is possible to allocate the resources directly, and to lay down from above the proportion of labour and materials for each channel of production.

But again, because of the limited resources available to them, the only way to direct resources into investment was to take them away from the work on which they were previously engaged, which was, in many cases, the immediate job of drawing a living from the land.

Even if the agricultural sector of the economy had not met with the setback it did, it cannot be denied that the planners gave to the building up of heavy industry a priority and a proportionate share of the labour resources which inevitably meant that the living standards of the people had little opportunity to rise for a long period. This was a conscious and deliberate decision by the Government to hold down consumption in the present despite the already low standards. The direction of labour into industry which was involved was responsible for a much faster movement from agriculture than would have taken place in a free market, since Russian industry, in its not very advanced state, could not have offered very high wages.

The Soviet path to development has been in many ways the reverse of those we have studied earlier. With Britain and America scarcity was removed by the productive ingenuity of countless individuals each working in his own way and primarily for his own satisfaction and reward; in Russia scarcity led to strict control and rationing of resources in order that certain priorities laid down by the rulers might be observed. Russia has certainly developed more rapidly than either Britain or America, who had leisure to proceed in the earlier stages at an unforced pace; yet one of the fascinating speculations of history is at what rate Russia might have advanced had political and social circumstances been different, and a liberal parliamentary democratic régime after 1918 had been open to the rest of the world and its capital. But events took a different course; and there is no doubt that both the Western and the Russian stories of development have valuable lessons for each other and for the emerging countries. In the briefest possible terms, the Soviet Union has shown the immense progress which can be made when a plan for developing the resources of a nation, prepared with the aid of all the best brains of the country, is backed by the energy and hard work of the people; on the other hand, the disastrous early failures in agriculture show the limitations of that method when decisions at the top are too rigid and take too little account of the need to carry the enthusiasm and support of the people.

III. Japan

In some ways both the most remarkable and, for us, the most significant story of development is that of Japan. Here is a country far removed from the European scene, a people of Asiatic race and one which until quite recent times was shut off from the outside world. For two hundred years from 1636 the Japanese people had been forbidden to travel abroad and foreigners were excluded from the country. Then in 1853 Commodore Perry sailed his American fleet into Uraga Bay and forced the Japanese to accept an "open door" trading policy and to allow the establishment of American consulates.

After some years spent in power rivalries between the noble families, a decision was taken in 1868 to adopt Western forms of government and to "seek for knowledge throughout the world". Four years later the first Japanese railway was opened; and foreign advisers and experts were brought in to help establish modern systems of education, banking and so on.

This conscious policy of modernisation and development in the fields of economic and social institutions provides the first real example which history shows of large-scale economic development by a previously backward Asian or African nation. Technical assistance was welcomed and foreign experts brought into the country as well as Japanese sent to study abroad.

While Japanese development in recent years has been remarkable in its extent, it should not be forgotten that quite considerable strides were made in this early period of the late nineteenth century. The crushing military defeat which Japan inflicted on Russia in 1905 was indeed a sign that in at least some respects her technical progress had already outstripped that of the empire of the Czars. Japan has, in fact, been developing fairly consistently for a hundred years.

The early period of Japan's return to the world laid very firm foundations for the subsequent advance. Docks, telegraphs, banks, medicine, engineering and education were already being planned on modern lines under the supervision of the foreign advisers even before the Emperor determined in 1881 on a transition to parliamentary government.

Particular mention should be made at this point of the emphasis which was placed in this early period on education. As early as 1872 compulsory education was instituted in a plan which called for no fewer than 54,000 elementary schools. The result was that as industrialisation spread there was a literate population which could cope with the problems which accompany it. There were men with enough knowledge of science and technology to run the factories, and an educated class for the jobs of administration. The foundation for the educated and trained modern society of Japan was laid nearly a century ago.

The technical aid received from abroad was considerable, and illustrates that in modern times some short cuts to development can be made; Japanese industry did not have to go through the process of inventing techniques for itself any more than did the Russians.

Nevertheless, the popular picture of the Japanese as merely good imitators is none too accurate. Of course they imitated the technical advances of the West; this was the way to wealth and they followed it. But in many ways they have maintained a marked individuality as a nation, and some of those distinctive national characteristics have been no less important to their development than the skill with which they copied Western techniques and models.

For example, although they adopted the forms of Western representative government, the real power in the country remained with a comparatively few leading families. These families had been the original feudal nobility; when the Emperor sent out his envoys "to seek for knowledge" the same families remained in power; but from being a ruling class within a feudal society they became within a generation the leaders of a rapidly modernising capitalist society. It has been said that "Japan stepped from feudalism into capitalism omitting the laissez-faire stage and its political counterpart, Victorian liberalism" (E. H. Norman, *Japan's Emergence as a Modern State*); and in the last chapter of this book mention is made briefly of the feudal spirit which exists even in the modern factory. These families, however, did not possess a great deal of capital, and most of the funds for building up industry in the first place were provided by the Government. One of the most outstanding aspects of the Japanese achievement is the speed with which capital funds were made available for investment in the basic structure of heavy industry, communications and the other requisites of a modern economy. The Government did not borrow such from abroad, as it might have been expected to do, and thus avoided creating for itself a heavy burden of external debts and obligations. Its main revenue, therefore, had to come from internal taxation. Through a heavy tax on land it raised large sums at the expense of impoverishing the peasantry; and in this way much of the early development of the Japanese economy may be said to have depended on a similar process to that of the Soviet Union—a forced levy on agriculture to enable capital to be provided for industry.

At the same time, generations of Japanese workers had been used to a very low standard of living, and so very little of the resources were diverted to be spent on consumer goods, so that capital could accumulate rapidly.

In the early years of this century agriculture still occupied more than half the population. But the pattern of farming was changing; the heavy taxation of land was driving many of the poorer peasants away from the farms, and into the factories of the growing silk and textile industries, while the land itself passed into fewer and fewer hands. Heavy industry grew, but was still comparatively small. Unlike Russia and America, but like Great Britain, Japan had to import raw materials because of her own shortage of mineral wealth; and this meant that there must be an increasing export of manufactured goods in order to pay for them. The standard of living consequently remained very low. Nevertheless, the increase of industrial activity and particularly of exports during this period signified the steady progress that was being made.

During the First World War Japan, like America, prospered considerably, both by producing materials for the Allies and by increasing her share of the export market for textiles.

But between the wars Japan felt the pinch of a growing population living in a small territory with little natural resources. Her growth had been based on a skilful use of modest resources, a reliance on steadily increasing cheap exports, and a continued very low standard of living on the part of both urban and rural workers. For many years now she had been importing rice, the staple food; and this, like the raw materials, could only be paid for by exports or by the quite considerable earnings which came from the prosperous shipping industry. With the coming of the terrible economic crisis of the 1930 period, Japan suffered more heavily than most. Silk exports, of great importance in the balance of payments, were particularly badly hit. At the same time rice harvest failures at home led to great hardship. These accumulating difficulties were a factor in the Japanese aggressions which began in the 1930's, since it was partly discontent with home conditions which led to the political action and eventual seizing of power by the military extremists. The Empire conquered the mainland areas of Manchuria and was led on to an invasion of China; but Japan did not gain much economically by her conquests, since the Second World War came too soon for her to derive any benefit.

The achievements of the Japanese before 1939, though considerable, seem quite modest beside those of the post-war years. Yet the prosperity of this latter period would be impossible without the foundations previously laid. Since 1945 the Japanese have most clearly taken their place as a developed nation. Their rate of growth is now the fastest in the world; and the standard of living of the worker, though not yet comparable to that of his Western counterpart, is at last rising steadily. At $500 per head per year it is still much lower even than that of Soviet Russia; but it is estimated that in purchasing power the Japanese worker's wages are much higher than the actual figure suggests, and his "fringe" benefits of social insurance and the like are much greater than those of the Western countries.

In one year, 1960, the overall growth rate of Japan was 13 per cent. The level of pre-war production was restored by 1953, and in the next ten years exports more than quadrupled in value; the income per head increased nearly threefold in the same period. Despite the growing population food imports have been kept stable because of improved efficiency in agriculture. At the same time, Japan offers the one example as yet of a country faced with a problem of growing population which has taken positive steps to deal with it, and which has largely succeeded in controlling and limiting the rate of increase.

How has all this arisen?

Firstly, because of the foundations for growth which were laid beforehand. But since the war there have been special factors which have enabled the leap forward to be so great.

One quite material consideration is that under the peace treaty with the Allies Japan was not allowed to rearm; consequently she has no military costs to meet. However necessary defence may be, the drain on the resources of every other industrial country (except, in the early post-war years, Germany, the other main loser), on what is, economically, unproductive expenditure, is quite considerable. Over seven per cent of our gross national product in Great Britain is spent on defence; and in some important fields where there are bottlenecks or shortages the proportion is considerably more.

In Japan all the corresponding resources which we, U.S.A. and Russia spend on military preparations have gone into the furtherance of her peaceful productivity.

In addition, the Americans have invested a very large quantity of money in Japan since the war. The occupation forces themselves spent enormous sums, all of which went into Japanese hands, and helped to create a very favourable balance of payments and gave the Japanese all the dollars they needed to make purchases of raw materials, machinery and other goods abroad.

For the rest, the traditional Japanese qualities of hard work and skill, building on the foundations laid earlier, have continued to operate. Perhaps the only really remarkable feature of Japanese development is the extent to which it has depended on the patient endurance and capacity for hard work of the ordinary Japanese, peasant or factory hand. A wise decision taken a hundred years ago by the authorities to expand on Western principles paved the way; but Japan has had no major advantages since then. She has not borrowed vast sums from abroad; her lack of raw materials and limited land area has made the problem of feeding a growing population very difficult, and in this respect she has had a much harder task than either America or Russia. It would be a mistake to ignore the fact that standards still remain quite low in some respects; but that she has achieved so much is both a tribute to the ordinary everyday citizen of the country and also an encouragement to those who live in other parts of Asia or in the southern hemisphere.

Further Study

Comparative study of each of the three countries, together with Western Europe and the United Kingdom, will be profitable. The different geographical circumstances (Japan is unique in this respect) and historical backgrounds are most important. Comparison can be extended to more general social characteristics—prevailing ideas and philosophy, systems of government, family and community life, etc.

The Growth of the American Economy, ed. H. G. Williamson (Prentice-Hall).

American Economic History, H. U. Faulkner (Harper).

The Affluent Society, J. K. Galbraith (Hamish Hamilton).

Soviet Economic Development since 1917, Maurice Dobb (Routledge & Kegan Paul).

The Soviet Economy—An Introduction, Alec Nove (Allen & Unwin).

The Modern History of Japan, W. G. Beasley (Weidenfeld & Nicolson).

A History of Modern Japan, R. Storry (Pelican).

CHAPTER 5

Some Principles of Development

LET us now summarise the lessons we have learnt through a study of the history of economic development in four major countries or areas.

1. In every case development has meant a considerable degree of industrialisation. An economy in which peasant agriculture has been the prevailing activity has gone through a change which has meant that fewer people work on the land but produce more owing to mechanisation and improved methods; while the remainder of the working population are occupied in other ways, principally in factories or other branches of mechanised industry.

Note that there are two factors here, not just one; industrialisation enables the use of mechanical power to be applied to productive processes, which provides for a steady increase in the volume of goods produced per man-hour. But also there must be an increase in output in agriculture; else with the withdrawal of labour from the land into the factories there will be less food to go round. This importance of greater agricultural output alongside industrialisation may not always have been fully appreciated; and the failure of both the Russian and the Japanese farms to match the growth rate of industry in those countries—not indeed necessarily through any fault of the farmers themselves—is the reason why the people had to wait a long time before living standards began to rise. It is not an accident that the improvement of Japanese standards has only been noticeable in the last decade or two, which is the period when agricultural output has made particular progress.

2. To ensure development in the first stages the technical knowledge must be available. Britain's economic growth took a longer

time than that of the other countries considered, because, being first in the field, she had to develop the technical skill, the inventions and the application of scientific knowledge from scratch as she went along. In other cases, noticeably in that of Japan, quicker growth was possible because the developing country could make use of the already available know-how of other advanced economies.

3. At all stages of development a large amount of investment in the creation of capital equipment, heavy industry, power supplies, etc., is required, together with an investment in the shape of educational provision to enable technicians and scientists and administrators to be trained.

It may perhaps be stressed that this problem is particularly acute in the case of countries developing today, because the more modern the industry the more capital equipment it requires. Errors are sometimes made and over-investment takes place, in the sense that an elaborate modern industry is planned for a primitive country that just cannot live up to it—when the provision of a few simple mechanical devices which even illiterate peasants can use and maintain might do far more good at far less cost. But, unless the developing countries are to go laboriously through every stage in the same way as Western Europe did, there must be intensive capital outlay on, for example, modern roads, harbours and power stations; else they will never begin to make up the gap which separates them from the developed world.

4. The pace of development is slowest in the early stages. The first steps, getting off the ground, are the hardest and take the longest. Once the process is under way, the steadily accumulating stock of capital equipment and of trained personnel is its own assurance of continued expansion. At first living standards will rise very slowly; and if the problem of finding capital is not made easier by circumstance or by outside help forced saving of some form will be more or less inevitable.

5. In all cases except that of Russia development has been greatly stimulated by help from abroad. In the case of Britain, who was first in the field, it was in the main the expanding colonial market and the opportunities to grow rich through foreign trade; in the

case of the United States it was rather the reverse process, with capital and labour flowing in from outside to help industrial growth. Japan did not make use of foreign capital in the early stages of her development; but she gives us a very notable example of the value of technical aid in the very systematic use which was made of foreign advisers from the beginning; and the flood of U.S. dollars during the post-1945 occupation and the Korean War certainly set off the explosive expansion of the last two decades.

In the case of Russia help from the outside world was rendered impossible by the mutual hostility of Communists and non-Communists. A direct consequence of this was the need for the Soviet Government strictly to restrict consumption and to enforce savings from the people.

6. Hard work is a necessary ingredient. How this hard work is achieved—by threats, promises, or by the creation of a genuine national spirit in which hard work becomes the "done" thing—is immaterial; and the pattern has varied in different countries. But development has never come without it.

7. From this derives a final point which is not unimportant. The people must want to develop. The sense of building a new nation which possessed the Americans in the nineteenth century; the fervour of the workers' revolution in the Soviet Union; the disciplined patriotic loyalties of the Japanese, all played their respective parts in the national growths. The climate of opinion was right in every case, and where it is not, as with the Russian kulaks during the first Five-Year Plan, growth is to that extent held back.

This point is true in a wider context than just that of willingness to work, and may be illustrated from the history of Western Europe. As we have seen, for many years the truths of the universe, even on the physical side, were believed to be obtained from theology and philosophy rather than from science; and until the acceptance widely of modern scientific method development was fundamentally restricted. In some parts of the world today superstitions, religious beliefs and traditional ways of conduct may be obstacles to development. These often age-old ways of life and belief cannot and must not, particularly if they are deeply ingrained in a people's conduct and social habit, be ridden over roughshod; but they must all the same be recognised as potential limitations on the speed of development. Summarised still more concisely and generally, four principles are seen as common to all examples of development:

1. Increased agricultural productivity.
2. Technical know-how and education generally.
3. Capital for investment.
4. A population which welcomes development and is prepared to work hard for little reward for a time.

There remains one additional factor to which this book, with its necessarily generalised approach, can make only passing reference, but which should nevertheless be constantly borne in mind when individual countries or areas are being considered. This is the factor of geography.

Britain had coal and iron at the right time and was well placed for overseas expansion. America's vast open spaces were to her a great natural advantage. Russia, too, has the mineral and agricultural strength to be self-sufficient and the wide territory of Asiatic Russia in which to expand. Japan has good ports to encourage her profitable shipping and trading development, but little else in the way of geographical advantage. All—and this may be significant—lie at least partially in the temperate climatic zone, where hard work is bearable, rewards do not come too quickly to encourage laziness, and where the seasons differ in character and therefore encourage adaptability.

Clearly every country has its own particular set of geographical circumstances which will affect the nature of its development; and some will inevitably have disadvantages in this or that sector. There is, however, little reason to assume that these variations are so great as to make it a surety from the facts of geography alone that some areas must always remain in an undeveloped state, except the most arid deserts and the polar regions. And under the advance of science even these regions can be rendered habitable and productive.

Let us now recapitulate the position in which we, as citizens of the world, find ourselves in the 1960's.

Of the three thousand million or so inhabitants of this planet less than a third belong to those countries whose development we have traced and who share the wealth and amenities which have been created.

Most of the rest of the world still exists in a poverty little different than their condition for centuries past. Illiteracy, disease and malnutrition are their heritage; famine is never far away, and the women know that of the children they bear many will not survive the first years of infancy.

The main difference between the present and the past for these people is that a growing number of them realise that such conditions need not continue; they know that many of their fellow-humans have found a way out, and they are determined to do the same.

The rest of this book is concerned with a discussion of one aspect of this way out—the aspect which should be of most interest to us in the West.

It is not proposed to examine separately the development of individual countries. Every one of them, as we have already stated, has its own special problems based on climate, social conditions, raw materials, geographical position, political influence and so on. Each of them will have to adjust itself in its own way to the four main principles of development which are summarised above.

Our concern here is to give particular attention to the part which international aid is playing in assisting these emerging peoples to help themselves. Such aid is inevitable and right, for two main reasons. Firstly, as we have seen, the history of developed countries suggests that help from abroad, in the form of technical aid, or capital, or the provision of markets for the growing exports of developing countries, can do much to enable these people to avoid the worst sufferings and hardships which may otherwise accompany the first stages of development. This should be clear from an understanding of the previous chapter.

To this is added a second important point. The present situation is an unparalleled one. We are not observing the slow and leisurely growth of communities with time to spare, nor are we seeing the development of comparatively limited and isolated pockets of the world's people. What is taking place now is an attempt by governments representing something like two thousand million people—the bulk of humanity—to throw off the chains of poverty and to follow in the footsteps of Britain, America, Russia and Japan. This is such an enormous undertaking that it quite clearly calls for the mobilising of the world's resources, and makes nonsense of any attempts by isolated groups—unless maybe they are of the sheer size of Communist China—to operate without regard to the rest of the world. And so, while realising that this is only one aspect of the subject of economic development today, we propose to look now at what is happening in the international community to aid the economic growth of the developing countries.

Further Study

This chapter summarises very broadly the main findings on the theory of development. Those anxious to go deeper into the economic theory should read *The Theory of Economic Growth*, by W. A. Lewis (Allen & Unwin), but it is not light reading. Still more academic is *The Stages of Economic Growth*, by W. W. Rostow (Cambridge University Press).

A useful exercise would be to assess the particular advantages and disadvantages of each main country or region—climatic conditions, absence or presence of raw materials, degree of political stability, the national spirit. (Israel is an outstanding and unique example of an underdeveloped *region* suddenly populated by a largely developed *people* seized with intense national determination.)

Some books on particular areas are:

Short Introduction to The Economy of Latin America, F. Benham and H. A. Holley (Oxford).

Studies in Economic Development, A. Bonne (Routledge & Kegan Paul) (India and S.W. Asia particularly).

Emergent Africa, "Scipio" (Chatto & Windus).

The Economic Development of Communist China 1949–60, T. J. Hughes and D. E. T. Luard (Oxford).

PART III

Towards a Developed World

CHAPTER 6

International Aid

In 1949 Harry S. Truman made his Inaugural Address to the United States Congress after his re-election as President. In it he called for "a bold new programme for making the benefits of our scientific advances and industrial progress available for the improvement and growth of under-developed areas . . . a co-operative enterprise in which all nations work together through the United Nations and its Specialised Agencies wherever practicable . . . a world-wide effort for the achievement of peace, plenty and freedom. . . . Our aim should be to help the free peoples of the world, through their own efforts, to produce more food, more clothing, more materials for housing and more mechanical power to lighten their burdens."

Shortly afterwards a less publicised speech was made by Trygve Lie, then Secretary-General to the United Nations. Proposing a ten-point "Programme for Peace", Mr. Lie in his sixth point called to the members of the United Nations to co-operate in a "new enlarged programme of technical aid to underdeveloped territories".

The Truman doctrine as set out at Washington became known as "Point Four", because it was the fourth of his main proposals. Mathematicians know that point four and point six make one; and it may be claimed, though with some reservations which will appear later, that these two themes are indeed one and are increasingly being seen as one throughout the world—the establishment of a world-wide programme of aid both in and out of the United Nations to help the development of the less fortunate or successful two-thirds of mankind.

Aid of this kind is no new thing; it has been going on for centuries. Every intelligent missionary has given aid to backward peoples; although saving their souls might have been his main purpose, he would know that curing their physical ills and teaching them to read was an equal part of the service he could render them. Imperial powers like Great Britain may well be accused of having used their colonies primarily for purposes of self-enrichment and military power; but incidentally they have given a good deal in the shape of modern techniques and skills, and in some cases more.

But nothing in the nature of a systematic world-wide attack on mankind's old and real enemies has ever been envisaged before—mainly because not until now has it been possible to consider such a thing. Both the increase of scientific knowledge and the shrinking of the world through faster travel and better communications have now made direct and unified action possible. Arnold Toynbee, whose breadth of historical view has given him an eminent position among scholars, has said that, when the history of the twentieth century comes to be written, it may well be said that the greatest event of the mid-century was, not the discovery of how to harness atomic power, but rather the discovery that for the first time it was now possible for men throughout the world to work together to utilise its resources in a common effort against hunger, disease and want.

The developing countries themselves have realised this, and no one can deny the spirit of change which animates the new nations of Africa and Asia. This spirit is in some countries mainly confined to the small proportion of educated men who have been abroad and seen conditions elsewhere, and who have read their economics, their history—and, often, their Marx. But these are the leaders who are determining the policies of their country, and every day as education spreads more and more are coming to share their leaders' views on this issue.

As a result of this most developing countries have already formulated plans for development. Not all of them are of the elaborate nature of the Indian Five-Year Plans, the third of which is now in operation, and none of them outside Communist China calls for such comprehensive mobilising and direction of the whole nation's resources as the Plans through which the Soviet Union carved its way to development. Most of them assume a considerable degree of external aid of one form or another. In the years since President Truman made his "Point Four" speech a great deal has been achieved. In a way this achievement is at the moment largely a psychological one. Despite all that has been already done, the income per head in the backward countries makes very little upward movement; the Indian villager still lives on the edge of starvation, the Bolivian peasant is still illiterate. Some of the countries may be a little nearer take-off, but the visible change is small at present.

In mental attitude, however, there is a real and quite significant change. In those advanced countries which must be the source of most of the external assistance which the have-nots receive, there is now a much greater understanding that the world problem of want exists; that the gap between the standards of living of the average Westerner and that of the African or Asian villager is intolerable and must be narrowed. To have attained this realisation is no small achievement.

But to recognise that there is a problem is one thing, to understand what is needed in order to solve it is another. We put our half-crown in the Oxfam collecting tin, and respond with generosity to the Freedom from Hunger appeal for funds to help an Indian village to irrigate its land so that more food will grow. We are aware of the darker side of the world in which we live, of the existence of depths of poverty and despair of which we are fortunately spared direct experience. But most of us have as yet little conception of the enormous scale of operations which will be needed if there is to be a real advance against want. Far too many of us are prepared to assume that this war can be won by private charitable contributions and that this constitutes the end of the responsibilities of the citizen of a developed and democratic country. In so far as we are all citizens of the world, this is manifestly not so.

Bearing in mind the size of this issue and the millions of people involved, to have established the problem is a first necessary stage;

the next is that more people should be aware of what needs to be done and the implications for all of us.

It would be very convenient if one could look at the present scene and be able to report a tidy pattern in which all development was proceeding according to a neatly co-ordinated plan, with each individual piece of aid and each item in a development programme fitting in to an identifiable place. But the world is not like that; the world is full of competing interests and competing views as to what should or can be done.

An attempt at analysis therefore is an attempt to simplify a very complex situation, and must be recognised as such.

One may classify aid in two ways—according to the type of aid, or according to the method or channel by which it is given. Under the first classification one may say that most aid is intended to satisfy one of two needs, each of which we have seen to represent a basic requirement of economic development:

1. Technical aid, through the provision of expert advice and assistance to help spread "know-how".
2. Help with loans or grants towards some form of capital investment in the developing countries.

On the basis of the channels through which aid is given, one gets a division along these lines:

1. Aid may be given from private sources—very often from a business firm, but possibly from a voluntary organisation or even an individual.
2. It may be the result of direct agreement between two governments—this is usually known as "bilateral" aid.
3. It may be "multilateral". The various schemes of the United Nations, to be considered in more detail later, are the most common forms of multilateral aid; but there are a number of other international bodies which are concerned in this field.

To see what the various categories signify in practical terms, we may look at some of the aid being given by or from Great Britain. First of all, technical assistance. Britain is, because of her many decades as ruler of a colonial empire, in some ways particularly experienced in the provision of this kind of aid. It may indeed be argued that the best of the district officers in the old colonial service were a model of what technical assistance should be, for they were men who before all else lived in a community and got to know it, to know the local customs and how far they must be observed. Such an officer knew the limitations of the people he was dealing with, so that any advice or help he would proffer would be based on an understanding of the problem from their point of view; he would know, for example, that whereas it was easy to tell African villagers that they should boil their water to sterilise it, it was also easy for a Westerner to forget that fuel in an African village may be very scarce and involve the womenfolk in much hard labour gathering it; so he would understand if they continued to drink unsterilised water. He would be less likely to make the sort of mistake which comes from ignorance of local conditions—such as, for example, was made by foreign experts in Turkey who "persuaded some of the younger peasants to remove the stones from their tilled land; when the grain sprouted, the fields of the old men had a better crop, since, in that dry climate, the stones served the function of preserving moisture" (David Blelloch, *Technical Co-operation and the Development Decade*).

Not every colonial officer was sensitive or devoted enough to act as psychologist, social worker and technical assistant in addition to carrying out his duties of keeping law and order as laid down by the British Crown; but the system was one which has left us in the United Kingdom with an invaluable experience and technique in this field.

Today, however, the more usual form of technical aid may be seen in the request from an independent government of one of the developing countries for a specialist to be seconded to them for a limited period from his normal employment. He may be an engineer, a farmer, a civil servant, a teacher, a doctor, or belong to any other of the many skilled and trained professions and occupations of the modern community.

The large number of different types of activity which can be classed as technical assistance makes it difficult to assess the exact total of those engaged in this work, but it was estimated that in 1963/4 somewhere around 16,000 British personnel were involved, not counting volunteers; and about 90 per cent of these were specifically employed by overseas governments. The Overseas Services Aid Scheme organised by what is now the Ministry of Overseas Development is an arrangement whereby British experts are paid by the governments of the territory in which they are working at the local rate for the job, and the British Government augments this amount to the level of the appropriate British salary scale.

The range of their activities is far wider than most people would imagine; doctors and farmers one can understand, but what about an expert in national savings? Mr. Henry Houston of Manchester, who graduated at the London School of Economics and an American University, was Regional Commissioner for National Savings in the north-eastern region of England. In 1962, "long after he had expressed an interest in serving the United Nations abroad, he was startled to receive a message from a colleague that 'three Thai gentlemen have come into my office and want a word with you.' The word was that they had chosen him, from among other U.N. candidates, to be the chief adviser to their Government Bank. The U.N. cable of confirmation arrived simultaneously. At the age of 57 when Mr. Houston admits he 'had been thinking of retirement', he found himself on the way to Bangkok and a completely new challenge."

Since that time Mr. Houston has advised the Bank on stimulating savings, on investment in development projects, and in many aspects of banking administration; he has also helped to arrange training for key officials.

Mr. Raymond Howard-Goldsmith returned from Niger in 1963 from a two-year assignment during which time he advised the Government of Niger on the development of their mineral resources and helped to establish a tin-mining industry. Mr. D. C. Robinson, a town planner, with experience as a senior town planning officer in Ghana, has joined a team to prepare a development plan for

Trinidad and Tobago; his task is to advise on land and building development.

These are random selections which help to illustrate the range of this work; but not all the requests are for experts at this top level. The columns of the educational press, for example, bear evidence every week of the demand for teachers in the newly independent states of Africa and elsewhere; and those who accept a post of this kind are contributing to the work of technical assistance. The traffic is not just of experts from England to the developing countries; there is also a movement in the reverse direction. Every university and college of technology in this country has its quota of students from Nigeria, Ghana, Pakistan, India, the Middle East; and this aid is far from being confined to the undergraduate level. Some of the most valuable jobs are being done in respect of graduates or men and women holding responsible positions in their own countries who have been sent to this country on a fellowship or scholarship to study the latest techniques and thinking in their particular fields. Thus:

"Mrs. Thecla Grace Mchauru . . . was selected for a UN fellowship because her country—Tanzania—needs better community services. Mrs. Mchauru was a Government community development officer, specialising in home economics and extension. Before that she had been a nurse, midwife and teacher. Her Government wanted to prepare her for greater responsibility, and enlisted the help of the UN. The UN sent Mrs. Mchauru to the Bath College of Domestic Science in the United Kingdom for a full year, and then to Denmark and Sweden for a tour of observation of their community programmes.

"Back home in 1963, Mrs. Mchauru was placed in charge of the women's section of a Community Development Training Centre in Northern Tanzania. In mid-1964 she is scheduled to become the first principal of a new training centre for girls in this area."

(Both the last two quotations are from Technical Assistance Newsletters issued by the U.N. Office of Public Information.)

The second principal category of aid is investment aid; and here again the range is enormous. It includes great engineering or building schemes assisted by government funds or undertaken by the large industrial combines; and at the other end of the scale it must include the kind of project which has been sponsored by voluntary organisations such as co-operated in the Freedom from Hunger Campaign. For most of the action initiated through that Campaign was designed directly as investment, and not just as short-term relief.

An interesting example of a private commercial firm collaborating with a voluntary organisation may be cited. The tractor firm of Massey Ferguson undertook to set up a farm mechanisation training centre in West Africa with the object of training instructors, farm machinery workshop personnel and master mechanics and to arrange for special courses for technicians concerned with farm mechanisation. This project was accepted by the United Kingdom Freedom from Hunger Committee as one of their approved projects. Through this scheme one of the greatest obstacles to the successful utilisation of modern agricultural machinery in West Africa, the lack of trained operators and of maintenance and repair staff, would be tackled.

In contrast to this small but valuable project one may instance the great Indus Basin Development Fund. Despite the political friction which has existed between India and Pakistan, each of whom makes use of the waters of the River Indus, U.N. officials were able to obtain a treaty between the two countries on the question of sharing the waters, and in 1960 the Fund was set up to finance the development of the river basin. The cost of this is being shared among a large number of countries, and the United Kingdom has agreed to contribute £21 million out of a total estimated at not less than £382 million. This is one of the outstanding examples of multilateral aid.

Passing now to a few brief notes on British aid considered from the point of view of our second classification, that of the channel through which it is given, it is probably unnecessary to give further specific examples, as the preceding pages should have provided adequate testimony of the type of operations carried out.

Since private business is run for a profit, the directors of big industrial concerns will primarily only be interested in schemes which will be likely to produce a return on their money within a reasonably short period of time. Although this leads to the exclusion from their sphere of action of many of the most necessary projects, yet the contribution made by private industry in development plans must not be underestimated. There is sometimes a certain opposition among the developing nations to overseas private firms, since they are naturally mindful of the extent to which exploitation of cheap native labour has sometimes marked this activity in the past. Moreover, if the private enterprises, having developed some natural resource such as oil, rubber or copper in the country then proceed to take out of the country back to their own shareholders all the wealth created by the development, there is no benefit to the "developees" and indeed a possible disadvantage through having had their traditional ways of life upset for no gain. Nevertheless, there is a very real part which has been played in the past and must necessarily continue to be played in the future by the privately owned business concerns. The activities of the oil companies in Kuwait, for example, have, to the knowledge of all of us, brought very great wealth to that little country. It is immaterial at this point to reply that most of that prosperity has gone into the hands of a few rich sheikhs—the problem of internal distribution of wealth created by development is a different, if highly important, subject. But Kuwait stands as the most sensational example of how foreign private enterprise can enrich a primitive community.

The sort of by-products which do result from the activities of private companies in developing countries include education and training facilities, the building of roads and houses and health programmes. Private business, too, has today a quite reasonable record of re-investing its earnings back into the developing lands; often more than half the return on the capital is ploughed back and therefore goes to provide more funds for further development.

Nowadays, with the march to independence of so many African and Asian countries which were previously of colonial or semi-colonial status, the outlook for private firms has in some respects changed. No longer can they expect the kind of concessions which, with the aid of a few gunboats from their parent and protecting government, will give all the gain to the outside developers. On the contrary, the danger is nowadays that firms may be discouraged from investment by the fear of building up assets and enterprises only to have them seized without compensation by an over-nationalistic government.

It is necessary today, therefore, for the conditions and terms of private aid to developing countries to be clearly agreed in advance, both to ensure that a fair proportion of the wealth created remains in the country, and also, on the other hand, to safeguard the interests of the firms concerned. Provided an agreement reasonable in this way to both sides is achieved, the part of private industry in helping the poorer peoples of the world in their fight for better conditions is very considerable.

There are, however, as we have said, many things which private enterprise cannot be expected to do. A newly-emerging nation requires many things which cannot be measured in terms of cash profits. Even in advanced countries, where the resources of the community are considerable and there are an established centralised government and social service structure, it is often difficult for schools, hospitals and roads to attract their fair share of the national budget. In countries with much more limited resources and often a fearful lack of trained public administrators these things will be even harder to come by without help from outside.

Consequently some of the most valuable assistance which the newer nations can have is to help their efforts to provide this type of capital investment. Harbours, power stations, irrigation works and the inevitable schools and universities are necessary conditions of economic growth. But they give no immediate financial return which can be measured by an investor or shareholder, and consequently do not attract private capital.

To help finance such schemes, therefore, British aid normally comes from the Government. And here it can take one of the two forms already mentioned—direct bilateral aid, or aid through an international agency.

In the first category one may instance most of the help which Britain gives to its former colonies and to those territories which are still dependent. It is by far the largest section of government help;

in 1966/7 aid to Commonwealth countries amounted to £165 million, divided almost equally between colonial territories and independent Commonwealth nations. Countries outside the Commonwealth received in the same period through bilateral aid a total of £21 million.

The sort of projects aided in this way by the Government include grants for land settlement of Africans in Kenya and the construction of a new civil air terminal in Cyprus; a loan to Sierra Leone towards the cost of a hydro-electric scheme, and loans to help countries buy capital goods such as rails, ships, etc., from Great Britain.

It should be made very clear early in the discussion of aid that it is quite wrong to assume that the money which is spent on British Government aid is just given away and represents a complete loss to us so far as our own affairs are concerned. In the first place, nearly a half of this money goes in loans which in due course are more than repaid to us, since we receive both annual interest and eventually the return of capital as well. This is a straightforward business transaction; the borrowers find it convenient to accept loans on their own interest.

Even where grants are concerned, it has already been hinted in the last paragraph but one that these very frequently lead to purchases by aided countries of our own goods, thus increasing our exports. In fact some grants are tied to a promise that the money shall be spent in this way.

For a country like the United Kingdom which is concerned over its balance of payments problem this is a very important matter. A failure to understand how much of the money spent on aid returns in this way encourages many people—including some of those in government office—to assert that our aid expenditure should be firmly restricted or even reduced; whereas in fact it would be difficult to prove that the total effect of our aid programme was to any marked degree harmful to our balance of payments.

If it may be asked what is the sense of spending money in this way if it is coming straight back to us, the answer is that this is just one of the remarkable tricks which the money mechanism can work. Money can act as a pump-primer, giving purchasing power to those who do not possess it, enabling them to embark on programmes of developing their real resources which would otherwise be difficult or impossible. For example, a loan or grant to India enables her to buy plant or machinery for a steel works and thereby build up her steel industry.

What in effect happens in such a case is that, if the aid is in the form of a grant, the United Kingdom is making a present to India of the plant and machinery. But in the process money is transferred from the British Government, via India, to the workers and shareholders in the U.K. companies which have built the goods; and this gives them purchasing power with which they will buy the products of other British firms and workers. The "original" government money will have come from the taxpayer, it is true; but provided the money keeps circulating among us, and provided the machinery we export is not desperately needed ourselves, there is no great loss to this country.

Obviously there is a limit to this conjuring trick; but the limit is not to be found in tables of money figures, but in the productive capability of the human race. And so long as many of these are unemployed, or underemployed, or just unproductive because they are working under primitive conditions, this limit has not been reached.

Apart from bilateral aid, Great Britain contributes to a number of U.N. programmes. These represent a new chapter in man's history —for the first time an attempt to organise a concerted campaign in which all countries may co-operate. They therefore merit separate and more detailed treatment.

The U.K. Government contributed in 1966/7 £19·2 million to all multilateral programmes, which amounts to 10 per cent of our total aid expenditure; and this is spent on both technical assistance and investment funds. It is a smaller proportion of our national income than the corresponding figure for a number of other Western countries; on the other hand, one must remember that Britain has a special role to play within the Commonwealth, and undertakes direct responsibilities for help to Commonwealth countries outside U.N. programmes.

The British total of all aid works out at about 0·6 per cent of the gross national product—that is, the value of all the goods and services produced in this country. In the light of the suggestion above that much of this comes back to us in any case, the amount does not seem excessive, quite apart from the wider considerations both of the ultimate value to ourselves of, and also of any ethical justification for, assisting underdeveloped countries. But the question of the amounts spent on aid will be discussed more fully later in a consideration of the total world programme and its adequacy to meet the need.

Before leaving this chapter a few words might be said about a very particular form of aid which is of special interest to many young people—international voluntary service.

The idea that young men and women from the "have" countries might contribute to the narrowing of the gap between them and the "have-nots" by undertaking some form of unpaid voluntary service has received a great deal of prominence in recent years. A number of organisations like the International Voluntary Service for Peace, the Friends Service Council, and the U.N. Association have developed schemes of this nature. A considerable impetus was given to the idea in 1959, when a "World Refugee Year" was organised with, as one of its objects, the rehousing of large numbers of refugee victims of the war who, fourteen years after the conclusion of hostilities, were still living in miserable conditions in camps in Austria and Germany—often nothing better than old Army huts long since unfit to serve for human shelter. As part of the Year's programme many young people spent a month or so of their summer vacation working on the rehousing sites alongside the refugees, helping to build their houses which would replace the slums of the camps.

Shortly before this an organisation was established in England known as Voluntary Service Overseas, with the particular object of enabling young people to spend six months or a year abroad, usually in a Commonwealth territory, on some form of community service such as teaching.

In America President Kennedy, very soon after his election in 1960, formed the U.S. Peace Corps, which gave official backing on quite a large scale to the concept of international service. In England there was a feeling that the movement should remain more in voluntary hands, but the Government has given financial assistance to the organisations concerned in this work, and set up the Lockwood Committee to provide a central point for planning, and to allocate the grant.

The last few years have shown very clearly that there are large numbers of young people who are eager to give some form of international service of this kind. The main difficulty is that most of the really worth-while jobs which need doing require both a professional skill of some sort and also a longish period of service; and many young people can offer neither of these. The sort of service which was available and so readily given in World Refugee Year is, in the international sphere, comparatively uncommon, though there is much that can be done in this country in the field of race relations.

But the sole yardstick by which all international voluntary service must be judged is the intrinsic value of the work done to the recipients. So more and more the bodies concerned tend to think in terms of at least a year's service with candidates chosen for some kind of expert knowledge, and suitability of character as well. Thus, Mary Wilkie, of Ealing, who speaks Spanish and was trained as a social statistician at the London School of Economics, went to Bolivia under a scheme approved by UNESCO and sponsored by the Bolivian National Union of Students, to help organise a literacy campaign among the Indians of the poverty-stricken villages in that country; and found her first job was to organise a census among people most of whom did not even speak Spanish.

Andrew Karney went to help with the work of the vocational teacher training centres set up by the U.N. Relief and Works Agency for Arab refugees driven from Palestine. Josephine Baxter responded to an urgent request for two qualified teachers to go to Tanzania to train French-speaking refugees from the little African state of Ruanda so that these refugees could themselves become teachers.

The only real difference between this form of aid to the poorer peoples of the world and the professional kind of technical assistance which was discussed earlier is that Mary Wilkie and the others were giving their services whereas the T.A. expert is paid his professional salary; and though they possessed some special skill, they were young and without much experience in the application of that skill.

As time goes on the demand for service of this kind increases, and there is every reason to imagine that a day will come when it is a normal thing for young graduates, engineers and apprentices to spend a period of twelve months or so in one of the developing countries.

There is no doubt at all that such an opportunity appeals to the sense of both adventure and idealism which are to be found in most young people; and it is well worth while for governments and the United Nations to search positively for ways and means of making the fullest use of this potential reservoir of aid.

A specialist skill; the ability to serve for at least a year; an imaginative response to the needs of others who live in very different conditions; an aptitude for practical adaptation to unusual circumstances. These are likely to be the sought-after qualities; and there are many young people who possess all these. Voluntary service can only be of marginal assistance in the great world war against want; but wars are fought by privates as well as generals.

Further Study

The whole question of present-day development and of international action to assist it is a current topic of ever-increasing importance, and consequently the daily press, reviews, television and radio are constantly concerned with it, and books at all levels are being steadily published. To keep abreast of a subject where on the surface at least there is continual change, one should make regular use of some of the following:

Articles in political and economic reviews, such as *The Economist*, *The World To-Day* and *International Affairs*.

Publications of the Overseas Development Institute.

U.N. *Monthly Chronicle*.

U.N. reports.

U.N. *Statistical Yearbook*.

(All official U.N. documents are obtainable from the U.N. Information Centre, 14 Stratford Place, W.1.)

The books listed here are relevant to the subject matter of this and the next two chapters.

World III, A. Moyes and T. Hayter (Overseas Development Institute—Pergamon Press). Chock-full of facts and figures.

Economic Aid to Underdeveloped Countries, F. Benham (Oxford). Deals in non-technical language with some of the controversial problems that arise.

The Rich Nations and the Poor Nations, Barbara Ward (Hamish Hamilton). Based on a broadcast series—very readable.

British Aid, a series of pamphlets published by the Overseas Development Institute, dealing with finance, education, technical skills, etc.

The Attack on World Poverty, Andrew Shonfield (Chatto & Windus).

An International Economy, G. Myrdal (Routledge & Kegan Paul).

The War on Want, ed. G. Evans (Pergamon Press).

World Without Want, Paul Hoffman (Chatto & Windus). By the Director of the U.N. Development Programme, quoted in Chapter 2.

Common Sense About a Starving World, Ritchie Calder (Gollancz).

Our DevelopingWorld, L. Dudley Stamp (Faber).

One Million Volunteers, A. Gillette (Pelican).

The LopsidedWorld, BarbaraWard, has just been published in U.S.A., and should be available here shortly.

World Poverty and British Responsibility, British Council of Churches (S.C.M. Press).

Information about Voluntary Service Overseas can be obtained from British Volunteer Programme, 26 Bedford Square,W.C.1. Most of the voluntary bodies working in this field (International Voluntary Service for Peace, U.N. Association, Friends Service Council, etc.) have by now a long list of people who have served abroad and are willing to speak of their experiences. Similarly there are now in this country a considerable number of people who have spent a year or so of their professional careers abroad and can give first-hand accounts of the work.

CHAPTER 7

United Nations Aid

ONE of the aims of the Charter of the United Nations is "to promote social progress and better standards of life in larger freedom". Over the twenty years of the United Nation's life the implementation of this aim has increasingly been channelled into a combined operation; and although the machinery created for this purpose is sometimes cumbersome and overlapping, and although it is only very half-heartedly used, the story is an encouraging one and gives hope for the future.

It should be remembered that the United Nations is not the first world organisation to be set up to establish principles of co-operation between the nations. The League of Nations, formed in 1918 after the First World War, was never intended to take a very active part in economic and social matters; it was primarily a political organisation, and apart from the International Labour Organisation, its other activities in this field were of negligible importance. It is therefore clear, from the much greater significance given to such matters in the U.N. Charter, even to the establishment of the Economic and Social Council as one of its main organs, that the statesmen of the world had already begun to realise by 1945 the importance which economic affairs would have in the post-war world; and rightly so, since, as Lord Boyd-Orr told the General Assembly of the United Nations very early in its existence, "if you do nothing about the atom bomb nothing may happen; but if you do nothing about the world food situation a great deal will happen" —starvation and famine, and the political unrest which will inevitably follow.

The Economic and Social Council consists of twenty-seven*
member nations; each serves for three years, and nine* members are
elected each year. Major powers like the U.S.A., U.S.S.R. and
Great Britain tend to be re-elected each time, so that they have a
continuing membership. So far as other countries are concerned a
geographical and ideological balance is sought, and there are always
some developing countries from each main area of the world on the
Council, a certain number of Communist powers, representatives
of Latin America and so on.

Linked with the Council, but independent of it, are the "specialised agencies". They are independent in that they have their own
headquarters, their own budget and even their own membership,
which may in some measure differ from that of the United Nations
itself. Thus Western Germany, which for political reasons is not a
member of the United Nations, does belong to all the agencies; and
the suggestion that receiving your letters promptly is more important than world peace derives from the fact that the Universal
Postal Union has more members, than the United Nations itself.

Each of the agencies has been set up to provide machinery for
international co-operation within a particular field—food and agriculture (FAO), health (WHO), labour conditions (ILO) and so on.
In this respect they correspond to the various committees of a
borough council, but with the major difference that, in the latter
case, the council itself has the executive power to carry out and put
into practice the recommendations made by the committees. The
agencies report annually to the Economic and Social Council, and
an important role of the latter is the opportunity it gives for general
debates on the economic affairs of the world in which representatives from both governments of the member nations and also the
specialised agencies can take part. The Council, however, cannot
give instructions to the agencies; only their respective governing
bodies can do this.

This is perhaps the place to point out that the United Nations
itself and the agencies are the servants of the member states and not
their masters. They cannot compel a member to take any action of

* 18 and 6 until a change in the Charter rules in 1965.

which it disapproves (except, technically, that the Security Council of the United Nations has certain political powers of this kind). They provide machinery for nations to come together and agree to adopt certain courses of action, and also to help in carrying out such action; but each government can make as much or as little use of this machinery as it likes.

A list of the various specialised agencies is appended at the end of this chapter. It would occupy far too much space to give a detailed description of each one, but a paragraph about three of those which are most concerned with development will serve to indicate the scope of their work.

The World Health Organisation (WHO) is naturally one of the more spectacular. One of WHO's first projects was to embark on a campaign to eradicate malaria, which not only claimed 300 million victims every year, of whom 3 million die, but is so debilitating in its effects that wherever it is found poverty automatically follows, since the peasants are too weak to give adequate attention to their crops, harvests are neglected and fertile lands left uncultivated. The DDT campaign carried out by WHO has removed malaria from many parts of the world; and some years ago the Organisation called for extra funds to enable it to finish the job. This was made urgent by the fact that a breed of mosquitoes immune from the effects of DDT was developing, and only a complete elimination of the disease-carrying mosquito could succeed. At present 48 countries have been enabled to eradicate malaria, and in 55 others the campaign is in progress; WHO estimates that altogether 190,000 persons are engaged on this work.

WHO plays a large part in many technical assistance programmes designed to train health workers, midwives and nurses, all of whom are infinitely scarce in most of the developing countries. A world-wide anti-tuberculosis campaign, and action to improve mental health are among its other many activities.

If the World Health Organisation keeps people alive who would otherwise have died, they need more food. True, they may be healthier and therefore more productive farmers. But they still need the help of the Food and Agriculture Organisation. The object of this body is quite simple—to make two tons of grain grow where one grew before. It has helped Thailand by advice on the storing of rice as a precaution against shortage and to avoid waste. It has reduced the incidence of cattle disease, particularly rinderpest, through vaccination campaigns. It operates an international anti-locust organisation. It is helping maritime countries to develop their fishing industries. It has embarked on a "world food programme" to use the food surpluses which accumulate in various countries for the development of others; thus, it arranges for such surpluses to be used in school feeding programmes in the poorer areas.

"Since wars begin in the minds of men it is in the minds of men that the defences of peace must be constructed." This is the motto of UNESCO, the U.N. Educational, Scientific and Cultural Organisation. UNESCO is engaged in work to eliminate illiteracy and to train villagers and peasants in simple techniques which will help in improving local conditions. It has embarked on a major project to foster research to improve living conditions in the arid zones of the world—in particular in that dry belt which runs across North Africa to South Asia and which was once quite a major food-producing region, until man's ignorance and folly ruined it. Here new techniques are being developed in irrigation and in the use of wind and solar energy. It has another scheme which will assist the Latin American countries to put every child into school within the next ten years.

These few examples show not only what is being done but, perhaps more important, the scope of what could be done, and also the degree to which in the modern world international co-operation is necessary if we are to make the best use of our collective resources.

But it should already be plain that individual and separate action by the agencies is wasteful, since their spheres of work continually overlap. And over the years since the Truman and Lie speeches were made, a number of additions to the U.N. family have been made the general effect of which is to make it easier for aid programmes to be planned as a whole. Just as the Allies in both the world wars had to appoint a supreme and unified command before they could defeat Germany, so a unity of direction must be given to this even larger and more important job.

When the United Nations in 1950 resolved to play a major active role in world development, its first step was to set up a Technical Assistance Administration, which should be the United Nations' mechanism for passing expert knowledge and scientific skill to the "have-nots". The scope of the work of this body need not be dwelt on here, as in the previous chapter a number of examples have been given of what is implied by technical assistance.

Before long, as ideas developed and became more ambitious—stimulated often by the very success and by the advice of the technical assistance experts—bigger projects, projects needing large sums of investment capital, were mooted. But if such projects are to be effectively carried out, they must be very carefully planned and examined before they are embarked upon. To survey the requirements and the expenditure of resources which such major undertakings would call for is beyond the capability of the governments of the underdeveloped countries. Moreover, many of such projects concern more than a single state.

To meet this particular need the United Nations set up in 1959 its Special Fund. The main object of this Fund, whose Director, Paul Hoffman, we have quoted in Chapter 2, is to prepare detailed plans for what would seem to be desirable schemes of economic development. Examples of these are the surveys which have been carried out of the Senegal and Niger River Basins in Africa and the help which has been given to the states concerned to draw up treaties for the joint use and development of the river resources.

To have a blueprint which has been worked out by experts from many countries and many skills working in co-operation is of infinite value both to the governments of the developing states and to such bodies as private firms or international combines who may be invited to carry out part or all of such projects. It can assess how far a scheme is justified at all bearing in mind the limited resources. It ensures that when development does take place it is likely to be far more productive as a result. In speaking to the General Assembly, Paul Hoffman said "Give us millions and we will lure billions".

In addition to its surveys the Special Fund has given a considerable amount of money to enable developing countries to set up colleges of technical education; this, like the other work, is all part of the necessary process of establishing a sound basis in order that investment may be profitably used.

In 1965 the U.N. Assembly amalgamated the "Expanded Programme of Technical Assistance" and the Special Fund into one body to be known as the U.N. Development Programme. All the specialised agencies like FAO and WHO co-operate closely with UNDP, which is directly responsible to the United Nations.

But all the technical advice in the world and all the surveys and studies are useless unless in the end there is money to pay for the capital development for which in many cases they prepare the way. Here the Asian and African and other developing nations have been pressing in the United Nations for a long time for much more in the way of funds to be available to them—and not unnaturally the countries with the money have been a little more reluctant to provide it.

There was, however, already in existence the World Bank, a specialised agency dating from 1944. The Bank exists specifically for the purpose of providing funds for investment projects. It has a very high reputation and is in some ways one of the most successful of the U.N. bodies. Most of its loans have been for development purposes, particularly in electric power, transport, irrigation and steel. However, by its articles of government, it is bound to act on the normal commercial principles of a capitalist bank—(for this reason the Communist states do not belong to it)—and only to invest its money in what are regarded as good business enterprises; that is to say, enterprises which will yield a normal rate of profit so that interest and capital in repayment of the loan can be paid back to the Bank. The Bank raises some of its capital in the money markets of the world, and is committed to charge for loans a rate of interest 1 per cent in excess of that on which it borrows itself, thus meeting administrative charges and enabling a reserve to be built up.

Now we have seen that a vast amount of the development which is most urgently needed cannot by its very nature produce an immediate return in money terms. You cannot pay 5 per cent interest on the building of a school out of the immediate proceeds of that school, since these proceeds are intangible, consisting of the knowledge and skill of the pupils, and they will only "show a profit" in the sense that the community in years to come will be infinitely richer in trained personnel.

So there is a need for the developing countries to be able to get capital funds for these very necessary projects through some other means than loans tied to market rates of interest.

To meet this, the United Nations set up in 1960 an "International Development Association". This body, known like so many others by its initials, has the function of providing "soft" loans or grants for development purposes. "Soft" loans are those in which the conditions of repayment are made easy for the borrower; there may be a period of twenty years or so before any interest need be paid, or the rate of interest may be kept much lower than the market rates. In a good many cases, however, a country may find even such easy conditions an intolerable burden on its limited resources, and because of this IDA can make outright grants, in which case there is no question of eventual repayment.

IDA's normal method to date has been to lend sums for a period of fifty years, with no interest payment charged, and with repayment of the loan starting after ten years. Such terms are clearly impossible to obtain in any other way.

IDA works as a kind of subsidiary, or, to use the official term, an affiliate of the World Bank. This fact is an indication of the high reputation which the Bank has in the world today; although by its constitution it is unable to lend or grant money on easy terms, it was felt desirable that its experience and proved ability should be used in the establishment and operation of the new body.

IDA gets its funds, like the Bank, from subscriptions from member nations proportional to their wealth; however, of the money paid in by a developing country, 90 per cent may only be used with the consent of that country.

This does not exhaust the list of U.N. organs which deal with development. An important part is played by the regional Economic

Commissions—for Europe, for Asia and the Far East, for Africa and for Latin America.

As the need for co-ordinating the action of the various bodies and agencies has increased, a very vital part in the field has been played by the U.N. Resident Representatives. These are members of the Technical Assistance staff and are stationed in each major capital of the world where U.N. development work is going on. Their job is to ensure that everything is going according to plan, that overlapping is avoided by consultation on the spot, that the home governments play their part and so on.

Two important principles which lie behind all U.N. economic work should be stressed before we leave the topic, for they underlie the whole philosophy of aid.

Firstly, no aid is given unless it is asked for. A country must first approach the United Nations with a request for aid; this is then looked into, and, if it is a sound proposition, and if funds permit, an agreement is worked out between the appropriate agency and the Government.

Secondly, every nation receiving aid is expected to contribute to the work whatever it can provide from its own resources. Thus, if a WHO expert visits a country to demonstrate modern techniques of child welfare or ante-natal care, secretarial services, transport and other such facilities may be provided locally; the amount spent by the aid-receiving country may well be as much in cash terms as that provided by the United Nations. When the World Bank makes a loan it normally only finances the foreign exchange costs; that is to say, it will find the U.S. dollars or the German marks with which the borrower can buy machinery or other goods. Again, local costs, which may be half the total, are met by the borrower.

If we link this procedure with what we have learnt about the development of countries such as Russia and Japan in the past, we see how valuable the aid can be. It does not in any sense replace the effort of the people of the developing country; but it can ensure that, in the very difficult condition in which many of them find themselves, and at a time when over half the world is trying to pull itself up out of the slough of poverty, these local efforts will bear much more fruit, and the period of intense hardship will be eased and shortened.

The above description serves to show how, as the whole question of world economic development has come ever more to the fore, the United Nations has developed machinery for carrying out the second object of its Charter. Each new requirement has challenged the international community to devise a new means of meeting the need, and the international community has responded. But a mere catalogue of agencies, organisations, committees, boards and the like, makes dull reading and omits one vital matter. It encourages us to forget the important truth on which we insisted in the very first chapter of this book; that it is people that matter, and what the abstract phrase "economic development" means in reality is food for the hungry man, health for the sick child, rest from intolerable toil for the weary mother.

Intergovernmental Agencies related to the United Nations

Title		Headquarters
IAEA	International Atomic Energy Agency	Vienna
ILO	International Labour Organisation	Geneva
FAO	Food and Agriculture Organisation	Rome
UNESCO	U.N. Educational, Scientific and Cultural Organisation	Paris
WHO	World Health Organisation	Geneva
IBRD	International Bank for Reconstruction and Development (World Bank)	Washington
IFC	International Finance Corporation	Washington
IDA	International Development Association	Washington
IMF	International Monetary Fund	Washington
ICAO	International Civil Aviation Organisation	Montreal
UPU	Universal Postal Union	Berne

ITU	International Telecommunication Union	Geneva
WMO	World Meteorological Organisation	Geneva
IMCO	Intergovernmental Maritime Consultative Organisation	London
GATT	General Agreement on Tariffs and Trade	Geneva

Further Study

Most of the comments at the end of the previous chapter apply equally to this one.

More specific study of the U.N. aid programmes can include a survey of the work of each agency. WHO publishes a regular and attractive bulletin, and the UNESCO *Courier* is full of information.

The U.N. Information Centre, 14 Stratford Place, W.1, and the U.N. Association, 93 Albert Embankment, S.E.1, provide regular reports and pamphlets on the work of the United Nations.

Books include:

International Monetary Co-operation, Brian Tew (Hutchinson).

The World Bank: A Prospect, James Morris (Faber).

World Health and History, W. Hobson (John Wright & Sons).

CHAPTER 8

U.N. or not U.N.

Wᴇ have explained in some detail the machinery and the operation of the effort being made inside the United Nations to harness the common resources of mankind. But in financial terms U.N. aid is only a small fraction of the total amount of aid which flows to the developing countries.

Look, for example, at the position in our own country, already analysed in Chapter 6. The estimated expenditure for 1966/7 was:

Multilateral aid (mainly U.N.)	£19·2 million
Bilateral government aid	£205 million
Private industry investment (not all strictly aid) approx.	£197 million

The percentage of British aid going through the United Nations, therefore, is only about 10 per cent of all government aid, and half that if we include private investment. The figures for the rest of the world would not be so very different, though the proportion of multilateral aid increases somewhat, because a country like Sweden, with no colonial commitments, gives a much greater percentage through the United Nations.

An innocent person who had read the previous chapter might have pictured from the description of U.N. activities a wonderful story of co-operative effort on the part of all nations, with everything fitting into the pigeon-holes of a World Master Plan, all worked out by the Secretariat of the United Nations sitting in their offices in the New York skyscraper which is the United Nations headquarters. In such a plan all the segments of a great puzzle, both the plethora of organisations within the United Nations itself and also the multitudinous national and private aid-giving bodies fall into neat place.

Such a picture would be far from reality. While the idea of a united and planned world campaign against want and hunger is indeed a magnificent conception which has inspired and will inspire many to give unselfish service, there are many reasons why such a campaign is a somewhat frail thing at the present time.

The new and untried nature of much activity in the field of world economic development would naturally suggest some caution. Nevertheless, some general targets for development throughout the world which could guide both the givers and the receivers of aid could be of great value and could prevent much overlapping and wasted effort. The United Nations does in fact ask developing countries to plan targets setting forth their needs, and these could be tied in to what different developed nations were willing to provide.

But to make such plans succeed requires a greater degree of international co-operation than many of us are at present prepared to give.

It is only too plain to all that in the political and military fields the conception of a loyalty to international or world interests is as yet a very ineffective force, unable only too often to assert itself in the face of the much more strongly ingrained feelings of nationalism. And unfortunately governments and peoples do not suddenly become completely altruistic and co-operative when it comes to development aid. The forces of national self-interest and the battle for power still go on.

The motives for giving aid are in fact many. A genuine concern to improve the worst conditions of life from which so many still suffer is by no means the least of them; but there are many others. Private businesses are concerned with profit-making; this is only natural, but it may sometimes lead to a desire to follow one's own nose for quick returns which may not necessarily coincide with the first needs of the people in the developing countries. And governments are not necessarily any more altruistic.

There are two considerations which weigh heavily with any government contributing heavily to aid programmes. Firstly, both the Government and the electorate that it represents will want to see value for money. And rightly or wrongly it will often consider that it can do this more adequately if it has direct control over the allocation and distribution of its generosity—if it can avoid having to share the control with a lot of other governments and with U.N. committees.

This reason for giving aid directly, or bilaterally, is all too often backed by another even stronger motive—the desire to use the giving of aid for political objectives.

Now to wish to control your aid programme in search of maximum efficiency is one thing, but to use it for political purposes may have very undesirable consequences. It is inevitable that anyone paying out large sums of money or otherwise contributing of its generosity to less fortunate people should prefer to give to those who are his friends and who share his views and outlook rather than to those who may at any time bite hard at the hand that feeds them. And, since even the richest country is limited in the aid that it can give, some kind of discrimination may be necessary.

It is as a result of pressures of this kind that the amount of aid which is given by governments through direct bilateral agreements outside the United Nations is several times greater than that which goes through U.N. channels.

The machinery and institutions of the United Nations are so young that it would have taxed them very severely if they had been asked to handle all overseas aid; moreover, there are many established channels of investment, notably the links between advanced and developing countries in the Commonwealth, which should be maintained and expanded.

Yet the discrimination to which bilateral aid can lead can take the form of very real and regrettable political pressure. The United States, which has easily the largest and most generous record of aid given since the war can also show one or two notable examples of political interference with aid programmes. Financial assistance for the construction of an important steel plant was refused to India because India intended that the plant should be state-controlled rather than run by private enterprise. More recently dissatisfaction with Pakistan's closer relations policy with Communist China led the United States to suspend promised help with the building of a new airport in Dacca. All aid was suspended to Ceylon for some time because of disapproval of her methods of nationalisation.

Communist governments on the whole seem to avoid too much hamfistedness in their negotiations with developing states, but no-one supposes that the Soviet Union gives aid to buttress capitalistic régimes. And so the benefits of aid can, under bilateral conditions, be replaced by the creation of international tensions through the attachment of political strings; economic "spheres of influence" have caused military wars before now.

There are many controversial political problems connected with the giving of aid, much to the surprise of most of those who contribute their halfcrown to the Oxfam collecting tin, and this is one of them. There are many different motives involved in any human action, and when a Western democratic country decides to help an Asian or African government with a loan or grant, every individual concerned in the decision may have a different purpose in supporting it. The governments of the developing countries are greatly concerned with the conditions or terms of aid. They welcome aid from any source, but are suspicious of any limiting conditions which may be imposed. Their suspicion, indeed, may sometimes be greater than is justified, for most of them have only recently gained independence, and they are very sensitive of anything which is a reminder of the colonial status from which they have only lately escaped.

From the standpoint of the developed countries themselves aid "with strings" is a dangerous game to play. There are enough ideological and political causes of tension and danger in the relations between the Great Powers without exacerbating feelings by a misuse of economic power.

A further illustration of the tendency to go outside the U.N. machinery is seen in the establishment of numerous "regional" organisations for the purpose; or, alternatively, the moving into the aid field of regional bodies originally set up for a different reason.

The Colombo Plan began as a Commonwealth initiative in South-East Asia, though it subsequently added some non-Commonwealth members. It has been active since 1950, and done much useful work; but some of the bodies which have been set up in more recent years seem to be quite unnecessary in view of the excellent machinery which the United Nations provides, including its own regional Economic Commission.

There is, of course, another side to this coin; and it is reasonable that lending governments and private firms should feel able to count on fair treatment from the countries to whom they provide assistance. The fear that your investment or business may be confiscated by a nationalistic or Communist government is not an empty one, and may well discourage lenders from providing such investment funds.

A balance must be drawn; the right of a government to nationalise and take into public ownership any industry which it thinks fit cannot seriously be denied to it. But there is a distinction to be drawn between offering adequate and fair terms of compensation to investors and confiscating their holdings without any compensation.

The United Nations has been aware of this difficulty, and one of the earliest resolutions which the Economic and Social Council passed on the subject of development recommended that developing countries should "provide adequate assurances with respect to the treatment to be accorded foreign investors, without prejudice to their right to take any appropriate safeguards necessary to ensure that foreign investment is not used as a basis for interference in their internal affairs". But it has not been easy to find a satisfactory formula which will meet every case.

The danger to developed countries from nationalisation or confiscation is much less than the very real risk of aid being used by donors for political purposes. And it is worth commenting that no recipient country has ever as yet defaulted on aid provided by the World Bank. Even from the most sordid motives of self-interest such an action, offending as it would all aid-giving countries in one fell swoop, is improbable.

The conclusions of this chapter may be summarised thus:

1. There are at least two very strong arguments for urging that the amount of aid which is channelled through U.N. agencies should be a much higher proportion of the total. These arguments are:

(a) It becomes easier for the government of a developing country to fit such aid into its overall economic plan.

(b) There is no question of political strings being tied to aid through the United Nations and its agencies. The receiving countries themselves have a voice in the administration and mechanism of aid, and the United Nations represents no particular ideological bias and has no commitments to any vested interest.

2. In the actual circumstances of the world as it is today, however, such an aim can only be realised to a limited extent; and the bulk of assistance will no doubt continue for many years to come privately or bilaterally. Those of goodwill will try to see that this aid will nevertheless be given without limiting or prejudicial conditions which make it less acceptable to the recipients.

3. If the maximum resources are to be tapped, the developing countries themselves must show some restraint and, despite their natural wish to exert full independence and freedom of action, must be prepared to meet reasonable requests of donors for security for their investments and loans.

CHAPTER 9

The Mekong River Basin Project

PERHAPS one of the most interesting of all the U.N. schemes is the Mekong River Valley project.

At the time of writing, war has been raging in Vietnam for a considerable time—a war which has increasingly troubled the consciences of many in the western world, and particularly in the United States which is so closely involved. In other countries in the area, particularly in Laos, there have been similar though less bloody cold war conflicts.

Three of the four countries in the region, Laos, Cambodia and Vietnam, were until recently French colonies and fought a long war against their European masters. As a result of the 1954 Geneva Conference on Indo-China, the independence of the three nations was confirmed, and shortly after Laos and Cambodia were admitted to the United Nations. But Vietnam is still not a member, as that country has been unable to obtain for itself the settled conditions which would allow its people to choose for themselves a single government which could represent them. It had been arranged that elections should be held in 1956, but the unhappy division of the country prevented this.

Independence has indeed brought to all three states further political unrest and only comparative relief from foreign intervention.

Whoever wins in this situation, the people lose. The peasants cannot sow or harvest when soldiers fight over their land; the son may have to join one of the armies or guerilla bands; villagers may lose their whole possessions, their homes, even their lives as the war of ideologies engulfs them.

All this is happening to a people already poor to the limit of existence. Each of the three countries mentioned above, together with Thailand, which is the fourth state involved in the Mekong River Valley scheme, has an average income per head of under $100 per year. The Vietnamese peasant working in his paddy field for such a miserable return may well feel that the only foreign assistance he needs is steady constructive work to relieve his poverty.

All this is not to judge the issues at stake in the war in Vietnam, or in any other part of the world where Communism and its adversaries may meet. But, in the long term, nothing is as important to South-East Asia, or to the world as a whole, including the people of the Great Powers themselves, than some relief to the prevailing conditions of economic and social squalor in these regions. No political or military factors can by themselves meet the needs. The people may be fighting United States soldiers or Communist guerillas today; they are always at war with General Hunger.

It is in this sense that the Mekong River Valley project assumes great importance. The United Nations has been concerned with it since 1952, and the extension of the war in Vietnam has at least drawn the attention of many people to its existence. President Johnson has stated that it is the desire of the United States to give generous economic assistance to Vietnam and the other states in the region as a part of the process of bringing peace; the United Nations has already assured that all the plans are there.

Before considering any of the details of the Mekong Valley project it might be useful to look for a moment at that other river valley whose development has become something of a byword. "TVA" has, in the free world at least, come to be regarded as one of the first and best examples of how a government can, by providing a basic foundation of "infrastructure", promote the whole economic and social development of a hitherto depressed region.

The area covered by the Tennessee River Valley is about equal to that of Great Britain, and is considerably smaller than that of the Lower Mekong basin. Between two and three million people live there, and there is a wide variety of life and landscape from the Great Smoky Mountains to the flat red lands of the west. After the American Civil War its resources were exploited without thought for the future; in particular, the cutting down of the forests for lumbering led as always to soil erosion and the wasting away of the best land. Poverty was everywhere, and though the general level was not as low as it is in Indo-China, many thousands of families had to live on less than a hundred dollars a year.

"And there appeared no way out. Each year fifty-two inches of rain fell, swelling rivers into angry torrents, flooding the land and carrying away strength and fertility from the soil. The forests, so sadly thin and overcut, were further depleted by burning. Income was less than half the national average. Only two out of every hundred farms had electricity. In the autumn of 1933 over half the families in the highland counties were on relief; in one county the rolls included 87 per cent of the families. There seemed no protection against flood, fire or erosion—no alternative to further descent into squalor" (Schlesinger, *The Coming of the New Deal*).

A large dam across the river had been built during the 1914–18 War to provide nitrates for explosives. This suggested the possibilities that might flow from a systematic harnessing of the water of the river. George Norris, who was Chairman of the Senate Agricultural Committee, fought unavailingly for years, but when President Roosevelt took office in 1932 he was persuaded by Norris of the value which an overall plan for the region could have, and in the following year the Tennessee Valley Authority was set up.

Such a public "socialistic" corporation is not easily created in the States, but Roosevelt had instilled a new determination into the American people to take positive action for developing the natural resources of the country and for putting to productive work the millions of unemployed.

The Authority planned and built a system of dams to control the waters. Such control made possible the creation of power plants and the generation and transmission of electricity all over the area of the valley. The river was cleared and rendered navigable throughout the whole length of the Authority's control, and water was provided for irrigation. As a result the farmer could grow more crops; and the

Authority also planted forests to prevent further erosion of the soil. The effect of the Authority's achievements has been to revitalise the whole community, both in the country and in the towns. By 1941 TVA was supplying electric power to 425,000 households, and the sale of electrical appliances in the region was proportionately among the highest in the country. A decade later the Authority was selling electric power to the plants of the Atomic Energy Commission, and the valley was receiving electric power more cheaply than anywhere else in the States except in the Pacific North-West.

The River Mekong is the tenth largest river in the world; it rises in the snows of the Tibetan Plateau, which is the birthplace of many of the great rivers of East Asia. From there it flows for 2600 miles south and south-east through the extreme west of China and through Indo-China to the tropical heat of its many-mouthed delta in the South China Sea. For the last half of its course—the part known as the Lower Mekong—it makes its way through the states of Laos, Cambodia and Vietnam, and forms for six hundred miles of that journey the border between Laos and Thailand.

This lower basin of the Mekong is a vast area of some 236,000 square miles, five or six times the size of Great Britain, and includes almost all of Cambodia and Laos, half of South Vietnam and a third of Thailand; 50 million people live in the region, about half of them in Thailand; most of them are peasants subsisting with difficulty on the one crop of rice which they harvest each year from their paddy-field. Every year the river floods in the rainy season, every year in the dry season large areas of the basin look like a desert. Yet the flow of the river itself, bringing down the melted snows from the mountains of Tibet to the humid plains of the lower basin, continues throughout the year; if the river could be harnessed and become a servant of man instead of his master the flooding could be controlled and water made to circulate through the countryside all the year including the rainless season.

There is not a single bridge across the river.

Less than 3 per cent of the basin is irrigated; all of it could be.

PLATE 7. To assess its natural resources, Nepal needed a full survey of its geological structure. An expert loaned by the Swiss Government has carried out this work. (By courtesy of United Nations.)

PLATE 8. The United Nations at work in the Congo. The International Labour Organisation trains motor mechanics and drivers in pilot workshops throughout the country. (By courtesy of United Nations.)

PLATE 9. Technical assistance in the Andes. This simple machine introduced by a UNESCO expert cuts down the time for making a ball of twine from one day to one hour. (By courtesy of United Nations.)

PLATE 10. The El Novillo Dam in Mexico, financed through the World Bank. Its first object is the development of electric power. (By courtesy of United Nations.)

PLATE 11. Old and new side by side. The pylons are part of an
electric power transmission in the Damodar Valley of India, financed
by the World Bank. (By courtesy of United Nations.)

PLATE 12. A Canadian team surveying a part of the Mekong River in Laos. (By courtesy of United Nations.)

PLATE 13. U.N. experts at Sambor, one of the proposed dam sites in the Mekong River development scheme. (By courtesy of United Nations.)

PLATE 14. The Asian highway near Kabul. This road will span Asia from Turkey to Java—a distance of 7000 miles. (By courtesy of United Nations.)

PLATE 15. Special techniques for low cost houses, with walls made from rammed earth, have been introduced in Ceylon to help cope with the severe shortage. The sites have electric lighting and piped water. (By courtesy of United Nations.)

The potential hydro-electric power to be obtained from the river could be sufficient for all the needs of the 50 million inhabitants of the basin.

The fish that could be cultivated in the waters of the Mekong and its tributaries could do much to increase the meagre food supplies.

With a regular flow of water two or three crops of rice could be harvested each year instead of one.

But why "could be"? Why not "are"?

The purpose of the U.N. operations in the Mekong River basin is to transfer "could be" into "are".

The Mekong Valley is not the Tennessee Valley; but the parallel is clear. By its studies and reports the United Nations has underlined the parallel.

It was the regional Economic Commission for Asia and the Far East (hereinafter ECAFE) that first took up the task of assessing the potential of this undeveloped river. In 1952 the Secretariat of ECAFE published a preliminary study of the problem of controlling the river, and stressed the need for expert investigations. However, the whole area of Indo-China was at this time in the throes of the wars of liberation which were being fought against the French; and it was impossible for any action to be taken.

A year after the Geneva Conference of 1954 the newly independent states of Indo-China joined together with Thailand to seek technical advice over the Mekong development. (North Vietnam, the Communist-controlled area of the country, does not lie in the Mekong basin, though it would gain considerable economic benefit from any development. The Government of Vietnam in the present context is the Government of South Vietnam, at Saigon.) The United States International Co-operation Administration was brought in to produce a report assessing the prospects, and at the same time ECAFE carried out a further survey.

As a result of this a Committee of the four governments concerned was established on a permanent basis, with full powers to request aid and to administer it when received. It is this Committee which is now responsible for the whole project.

In 1957, at the request of the Committee, the United Nations sent a team of five experts to submit detailed proposals for action. The leader of this team was the Canadian engineer Lt.-Gen. R. A. Wheeler, who had only shortly before this earned considerable prestige as the head of the operations for clearing the Suez Canal after it had been blocked during the 1956 Suez crisis; the clearing had been accomplished in a fraction of the time which the Western experts had anticipated.

The report of the U.N. Technical Assistance mission stressed yet again the remarkable possibilities for development, and also the need for yet further detailed planning and collecting of information about water levels, amount of flow and so on. A sum of $9·2 million was estimated as the cost merely of collecting the data; and it is worth mentioning that this sum was equal to one-third of the total funds available to the Technical Assistance Board at this point of time.

Nevertheless solid action now began. The Committee began soliciting for contributions, and before long twelve countries had pledged or advanced sums exceeding what was required for the next planning and survey stage, while the United Nations itself had contributed over $3 million from its funds. Twelve U.N. agencies are now at work on the project, including the Technical Assistance Board, the Special Fund and ECAFE. Twenty-one countries have now become involved directly in some form of aid.

The basic scheme envisages the construction of five dams at different sites on the main river, each of which will provide power, irrigation and flood control; each will increase the yield of crops, and will allow through irrigation, at least two crops a year being produced instead of the one harvested at present. They will also make it possible for other crops to be grown, and they will generate a vast amount of electric power at low cost. Moreover, the dams will make it possible to improve the control of the river flow and render it more easily navigable.

In addition to the mainstream projects, ambitious plans for developing the tributaries of the Mekong have been prepared, and dams are already under construction or in operation in five cases.

A demonstration farm has already been established in the Vientiane Plain of Laos; FAO, the Special Fund and the Israeli Government are especially concerned with this. Rice is being cultivated in a section of 400 acres which has been specially irrigated and already yields four or five times the product obtained by local farmers on their rain-fed plots. Other crops have been developed with good results, and the plans include the setting up of other demonstration farms in other districts. Construction has started on several more projects.

Of the mainstream projects three have been given special priority. The largest is at Pa Mong, on the borders of Laos and Thailand; this will irrigate $2\frac{1}{2}$ million acres and produce 1 million kilowatts of electric power.

At Sambor, in Cambodia, another dam will produce power for industrial, domestic and lighting purposes in Cambodia and Vietnam; Japan is carrying out the principal investigations for this project.

Perhaps the most interesting scheme is concerned with the Tonle Sap River, because of the unusual geographical conditions. This river joins the Mekong at Pnom Penh, near the Cambodian–Vietnam border, and within the very large delta region of the Mekong. For five months of the year this river flows from south to north; for the rest of the year it reverses its flow, and runs from north to south.

The reason for this curiosity of nature is the irregular water flow of the Mekong itself. When it floods, the Tonle Sap acts as a relief by taking off some of the flood water into the Great Lake which lies nearly a hundred miles north of the confluence of the Tonle Sap and the Mekong. But when the level of the Mekong is low, the Tonle Sap reverses its flow and empties water from the Great Lake into the Mekong.

In the Tonle Sap and delta area there are a number of problems, one of the principal of which is the very considerable flooding in the delta. There is also an intrusion of salt water on to the land during the low water period, and this makes much of the land unfit for agriculture. The irregular water flow also makes navigation difficult for ocean-going vessels anxious to reach Pnom Penh; and, finally,

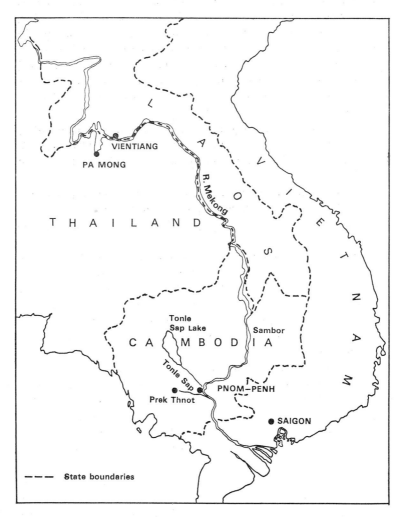

FIG. 3. Map of the Lower Mekong River Valley.

the drop in the water level which takes place annually in the Great Lake has an adverse effect on the volume of fish, on which Cambodia depends.

To deal with all these problems the Mekong River scheme plans to build a gated barrage across the River Tonle Sap so that the level of the lake can be regulated. The two-way flow of the river will be continued, but with a scientific control of the lake level so that while flood water is taken off the delta during the wet season, and at the same time water will be made available to the Mekong during the dry season, the lake will never be reduced below the capacity which makes it most suitable for fish cultivation, and the Mekong will always be deep enough for ocean-going vessels to be able to reach Pnom Penh.

The simple basic principles underlying these river valley schemes should not blind one to the immense amount of technical and scientific work which is involved in the careful surveys and estimates which have to be made and which, despite all that has already been done, are still continuing. Nor should one underestimate the magnitude of the eventual construction work which will have to be done.

The 1964 annual report of the Mekong Committee has as an Appendix a summary table of the proposed work programme for 1965, and this catalogues twelve major objectives including general planning, mainstream and tributary projects, navigation improvement and ancillary projects. These twelve objectives are subdivided into 110 subsidiaries, such as mineral surveys, fertiliser study, forestry and supply. Different organisations or countries are responsible for each of these; the United Kingdom is specially concerned with the navigation improvement.

The plan is a combined operation which is comparable with the most complicated military campaign; the human ingenuity which went into the preparation of D-day is rivalled here.

But those who planned the invasion of Europe knew that the whole resources of the allied world would be at their disposal, and that the skill and brainwork of the conception of the plan would be followed by the blood, tears and sweat of the millions who carried it out.

Can the same be said of the Mekong Valley scheme?

The Committee had at the end of 1967 resources contributed or pledged amounting to $160 million, and, although so much, including all the mainstream projects which are its core, is still only in the planning stage, over half of the current expenditure is now being devoted to actual construction, rather than planning.

1967 saw the Committee's funds increased by nearly a half over the total at the end of 1966, and a big new project initiated at Prek Thnot, in Cambodia, where the Cambodian government is itself providing one third of the total cost. These developments lead one to hope that the Mekong Valley scheme is really getting under way, and that the world is beginning to see that it provides the best answer to the instability of the whole of South-East Asia.

If we compare the $160 million now available with the U.N. estimates of the sums that will be eventually needed we get a picture of the magnitude of the task. In *The United Nations Development Decade—Proposals for Action* the following comment is made on the Mekong River project:

"A recent rough estimate puts the cost of building the first five mainstream projects, including tributary developments roughly equivalent in cost and results to three times the totals involved in the four United Nations Special Fund tributary projects and some navigational improvement, at about $2,000 million. This estimate includes the costs of construction of dams and locks, power houses and equipment, irrigation canals and pumping stations, etc., but not such ancillary investments as factories to utilise the newly available power, electrical equipment for farms, etc., which might be three to four times as great as the initial investment of $2,000 million."

It goes on to say:

"*The time scale.* Perhaps the most significant feature of the Mekong River project for the development decade is the time scale on which it is conceived. Already ten years have passed since the idea was first conceived, and as yet no actual construction work has begun. [This was written in 1962.] As early as 1959, the Committee envisaged that the completion of the first phase of the project might take twentyfive years, and outlined fairly detailed plans for the progress of development on a number of related projects during the first fourteen years, starting with five years of work on data collection. The full utilisation of the economic potential created by the scheme will take very much longer—and if it contributes to the initiation of self-sustaining growth in the area affected by it, may be said never to reach an end."

The Committee intends that such an international scheme shall be operated by an international administration. They are so confident of the eventual success of the scheme that they want the construction to be financed by loans rather than grants, because in this case nothing will be attempted unless it is clear that the benefits will outweigh the costs, and the loans can be repaid.

The project, like so much else in the U.N. economic programme, is a challenge to humanity. We can so transform conditions in the Mekong River Basin that the peasants of the valley need no longer live out their lives in conditions which should be a lasting challenge and affront to a world which claims to be civilised and to have mastered the secrets of science. This can be one of the growing points of the new world.

Further Study

The periodic reports of the U.N. Mekong Committee are obtainable from the U.N. Information Centre. A thorough study of the area—geographical, economic, social, etc.—will add depth to one's understanding of the U.N. project and its potentialities.

Other large international undertakings which can be studied are the schemes for the River Volta and the River Indus, and the Asian Highway project. Appraisals of each of these will involve a thorough survey of conditions in the areas concerned.

CHAPTER 10

Trade not Aid

In 1957–8 a total of about $4000 million flowed from the developed to the developing countries in aid.

But in 1957–8 there was a modest slump in trade in the United States—nothing remotely comparable with the depressions which led to millions of unemployed in the inter-war years, but enough to have some effect on prices. What resulted was that the prices of primary products—i.e. raw materials and agricultural products—which are the chief exports of the developing countries, declined by about 7 per cent, but the recession did not affect the price of most manufactured goods, which continued to rise.

The result of this was that, though the underdeveloped countries exported just as much of their produce as they did in the previous year, they got less money for it, while the manufactured goods they needed to import cost them more. The net loss to these countries was reckoned at $2000 million.

There is no sense in making massive efforts to assist the poorer peoples with grants, loans and services if at the same time the arrangements by which they trade with the rest of the world deteriorate so badly that they have to pay back half the total of aid received through a worsening of the conditions under which they trade. And the period 1957–8 is not isolated. It was calculated that between 1950 and 1962 the industrial countries more than doubled the proportion of their total incomes that they were contributing in aid—from 0·3 per cent at the beginning of the period to 0·7 per cent at the end. But the whole of this increase was wiped out by the loss of income suffered by the developing countries through the

116

worsening of the terms of trade—that is, by the relation between the prices received for their exports as compared with what they must pay for imports. The terms of trade have gone almost consistently against the poor nations since the war.

To make matters worse, in the meantime the interest payments due on loans already made are increasing, and add a further burden

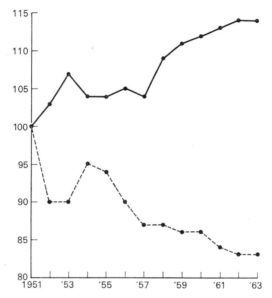

FIG. 4. Terms of trade (U.N. terms of trade; adjusted so that 1951 = 100).
——— Developed countries.
– – – – Developing countries.

to the developing countries; so that despite the growing amount of aid in financial terms these countries are effectively receiving less assistance than they did fifteen years ago.

The realisation of this rather staggering fact adds another important dimension to the conception of the world campaign against underdevelopment. Obviously the long-term objective is that all countries shall be self-supporting and independent of the need to rely on foreign aid; and this means that the poorer nations must not only produce more for internal consumption, but must increase their exports so that they can balance their trade by exporting sufficient to pay for all the imports they require. "Trade not Aid" is the motto heard with increasing frequency and it sums up the ultimate aim of the underdeveloped.

It is the main purpose of aid to provide initial help in the difficult period before take-off; but how long this period lasts and how long aid will be required depends on how favourable are the opportunities for an expansion of the export trade.

Clearly, then, anything which limits the capacity of the developing countries to sell their goods abroad, or which reduces the prices they obtain for these goods, is cancelling out the good done by international aid.

It was considerations like the foregoing that led the United Nations to hold, in 1964, one of the biggest and most important conferences of its history, the Geneva Conference on Trade and Development. Like so many international gatherings, this one did not itself produce any startling results, but it laid down some agreed principles and established a Trade and Development Board as a piece of permanent machinery to get on with the day-to-day job of putting these principles into effect.

In 1968 a second Trade and Development Conference was held at New Delhi. Since 1964 a lot of things had happened; but for the most part they were not the things that the developing countries had hoped for. No one could point to anything much that had been achieved by the Trade and Development Board. The have-nots were looking at New Delhi for deeds; but the developed countries were not forthcoming. Their own financial difficulties, their balance of payments problems, made them unwilling to agree to any proposals which might even temporarily cost them something. So most of the previously agreed principles were reaffirmed, and nothing much else happened.

This illustrates a growing and rather dangerous frustration between rich and poor nations. To close this gap, as an observer at

New Delhi commented, "layer upon layer of problems have to be uncovered and solved", and in this respect the 1968 meeting at least continued the dialogue.

What were the main topics which the two conferences discussed?

One of the major difficulties facing the developing countries is the fact that not only are their exports principally raw materials or foodstuffs, but very often each country depends on one or two commodities only for the greater share of its export earnings; a small reduction in price or demand for this commodity can thus seriously affect its whole economy.

In the rubber plantations of a certain Asian country production increased by 18 per cent in seven years; at the same time the value of the crop dropped by 14 per cent. Putting it another way, a drop in the price of rubber equivalent to one-third of a U.S. cent per pound had caused an annual loss of more than $5 million for the country. Similar setbacks might be experienced by an African exporter of cocoa or peanuts, a Latin American economy based on coffee or a metal, a Pacific producer of copra or coconut oil, or an island dependent largely on sugar.

This difficulty is likely to be aggravated in the future, because, as general standards rise throughout the world, the demand for food and other primary commodities becomes proportionately less. The percentage of a poor family's income spent on food is higher than that of a rich family, who when they have enough will buy no more however their income may grow; but their demand for industrial goods, for cars, refrigerators and washing machines is insatiable.

This fact helps to explain why the prices of the primary commodities are, as we have seen, tending to fall compared with those of manufactured goods. This is a fundamental fact which must be understood.

It is true that in the developing countries the demand for primary products will rise for a time as families are able to spend more on food and basic necessities. But this by itself will not help them to compete on equal terms with the developed countries.

So, the developing countries themselves must produce a greater variety of goods and must industrialise more rapidly. Most of them are in fact planning to do so, and much of the aid which, for example. India receives is devoted to the furtherance of her successive Five-Year Plans which, among other things, aim to achieve just this purpose.

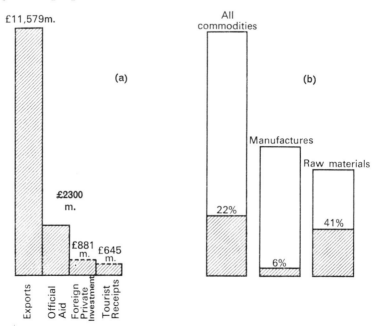

Fig. 5. (a) Developing countries' sources of foreign exchange. (b) Developing countries' share in world exports.

But the industrialised countries have a great responsibility to see that they help to provide the most favourable conditions for this end.

Every advanced country puts up tariff barriers against the entry of goods from abroad; and in general the restrictions imposed are greater on manufactured goods. Countries like our own must be prepared to reduce their tariffs against such goods if they come from a developing country, and to allow entry of these goods even though in some cases this may adversely affect certain interests among their own people.

This is a particularly important matter for the have-not countries; how can they build any industries if their potential export markets ban the entry of the products of those industries? For example, raw skins and hides are allowed by most Western European governments to enter without paying duty, since the European manufacturers of finished products made from these hides need them for their industry. But dressed skins and hides imported from abroad have to pay a duty. Thus the emerging nations are hindered from developing industry because they can export the raw material but find tariffs imposed on their finished goods. This situation obtains in a good many industries.

Not only, then, do we have the illogical nonsense of our government making a sizeable grant in aid to a country such as Tanzania while at the same time we increase the prices of the machinery which the Tanzanians want to buy with the money. We can also enjoy the spectacle of, say, a British engineer loaned to a developing country in order to aid them in manufacturing finished products from their raw materials; while the same government which provided the expert, or the funds to employ him, maintains a tariff which prevents the developing country from exporting its manufactures.

Quota restrictions have a similar effect to tariffs; the physical quantity of manufactured cotton textiles which may be imported from different countries is limited by law, which effectively prevents a developing country from expanding its export market by increasing its volume of exports of this type.

Advanced countries must refrain from using their powerful bargaining position in order to obtain favourable conditions and concessions for their own trade as compared with that of the poorer countries. Thus they should be prepared to give free entry to the goods from developing countries while accepting that the developing nations may impose restrictions and tariffs on the exports of the advanced states in order to protect their own growing industries.

They can, further, refrain from encouraging research on substitutes which might replace a raw material which is a leading export and money-earner of a developing country.

They can help to negotiate international agreements which will fix a stable and reasonably profitable price for the products of the developing countries. We have managed to obtain a high volume of production from our quite limited number of agricultural producers by fixing an annual price guarantee which ensures to the farmer an adequate reward for his labour, even though a fair proportion of this price may come in subsidies from the Government rather than directly out of the consumer's pocket. A similar practice has been used with profit in the international field, but much more could be done in this way to give guarantees to encourage an expanding and developing growth rate.

The advanced nations can agree that when they receive interest on loans which they have made to the developing states they will use these funds to purchase goods produced by those countries.

One can be sure that vested and sectional interests will be more vocal and resistant to new ideas in the sphere of trade than in most others. The changes which must come if serious measures are taken to keep the balance of trade moving favourably for the have-nots are all going to affect individual industries and groups of workers. Industrialists engaged in these affected branches, and unions representing the workers, are, if the past is any guide, going to be very forthright in defence of their interests. Yet the Government, and the people who elect it, must be prepared to consider wider issues, and to accept a much broader conception of the national interest which sees the value to this country, as to other developed countries, of a prosperous and stable world.

In the light of these considerations, the attitude taken in the past to such matters as the import into this country of cheaply produced goods from countries like Japan and India—of Japanese watches and cameras, of Indian textiles—needs thinking about. It has been widely assumed that we were justified in protecting our own industries by placing tariffs and other restrictions on the entry of such goods, with the direct intention in many cases of making it impossible for them to be competitive with our own products. And the argument has often been used that there was something almost immoral in this competition, in that the Japanese and Indian workers were accepting very low wages and undercutting our own highly-paid workers. But it is increasingly becoming realised that it is indeed only by such competition and by initially accepting what are to us low standards of living that the workers of the developing countries will ever make much headway in the world. These standards are, after all, no worse than the conditions in which they have been living for generations, nor are they worse than those which our forefathers had to accept in the first days of British industrialisation.

A new conception of what should be our attitude in these circumstances has to be reached. We must not prevent the poorer nations from increasing their exports to us; it is only in this way that they can earn the foreign money with which they can buy from us and ultimately improve their own standard of living. We must be prepared to readjust and replan our own economy in order to produce the sort of goods which, despite the higher costs of our own labour, cannot be produced more cheaply by the underdeveloped—possibly such commodities as need a high proportion of advanced technological skill in the making, which our people are more qualified to produce. Meanwhile, governments must help in the adjustment from one type of industry to another, and provide retraining and financial assistance for individuals who lose their former livelihood. Such a constructive approach will bring increased prosperity both to the developing countries and to ourselves.

These are some of the issues which arise from the U.N. Trade Conferences and from the "Trade not Aid" slogan of which much is heard at international meetings today. Since most of us are particularly susceptible to anything which affects our jobs and livelihood it is very important to have some understanding of these issues.

Certainly many people in the developed countries are just not ready for the kind of changes which some of the proposals listed above would require. And it is hard for a man who has spent most of his working life in, say, the cotton industry to be told that it is in his own interests that we should accept cheaper cotton goods imported from the countries of Asia, even if this means the destruction of our own industry. Yet this is precisely what we must say. The expansion of international trade and the discovery of new markets was one of the main causes of our eighteenth- and nineteenth-century growth. The new markets today can come from the growing incomes of the inhabitants of Africa, or Latin America, or Asia. They want to import, to buy our goods, but trade must be a two-way process; and the extent to which they can buy our goods is directly proportional to the extent to which we buy theirs. At present the dice are weighted against them; the UNCTAD Conference proposals are intended to shift the balance the other way.

The developed countries must definitely and deliberately refrain from using their bargaining power—the bargaining power of the strong against the weak—to the full. And we must remember, if we are to keep any sanity in this whole question, the two main points made at the beginning of this chapter—firstly, that we have been giving aid with one hand and taking it away through unhelpful trading terms with the other; and, secondly, that until the developing countries can earn their own way in the world by trade they will go on wanting aid.

Further Study

The amount of readable non-specialised matter on this subject is small.

It would be useful to study the imports and exports of individual developing countries, to see the proportion of exports consisting of raw materials or of one single product, and to compare present figures with those for some years back. But care needs to be taken when dealing with statistics; it is important to make sure that one is comparing like with like, and help from someone with a little experience of dealing with statistical tables is advisable.

It would also be valuable to look at British imports from developing countries, and to learn which of them are especially dependent on our markets.

Christian Aid has produced a whole series of pamphlets on aid, of which *Overseas Aid—The Role of Trade* (British Council of Churches, 10 Eaton Gate) gives a good introduction to trade and development problems.

The Less Developed Countries in World Trade, M. Cutajar & A. Franks (Overseas Development Institute) is a very detailed reference book.

CHAPTER 11

The Population Problem

WE have been discussing the ways and means by which the 3500 million or so of us on this planet can combine to increase the supplies of goods—food, houses, clothes—which so many of us so desperately need.

We have not so far given any very great attention to the fact that before the end of this century there will be 7000 million of us to feed, house and clothe.

But clearly this staggering population increase—not unjustly described as an "explosion"—constitutes perhaps the most important consideration of all in the struggle to fulfil the rising expectations of the underprivileged. (One may indeed go further and say that the rising expectations of the privileged, including ourselves, are equally at stake.)

To grow more food to the extent that is necessary to give the numbers now alive enough to eat is something that as yet we have failed to do; in the light of that failure, to have to provide for double the number of people even at the present inadequate level is a daunting task.

It is true that as the population increases, so does the number of workers. But as against this the amount of land in cultivation is limited, and even if you double the area of cultivated land because the number of people doubles you can only do this by taking in inferior and less productive land; and the same story of diminishing returns is likely to be true of most other things, such as mineral resources, fisheries, and so on.

The main burden of coping with this fantastic problem of feeding a world population which will double in thirty-five years must therefore be borne by the scientists, the technicians and the experts and by the application of their knowledge and skill towards gaining a vast increase in agricultural productivity per head and per acre.

The experts of the Food and Agriculture Organisation say that the job can be done; that provided—and it is a big proviso about which at present nobody could dare to be too optimistic—we are prepared to make this a first priority, we can so increase the yield of food that we can both raise standards and cater for the increasing numbers during the next two or three decades. But this will involve making food production a more important objective than armaments and defence, or sending a man to the moon; and so far the evidence that we are ready to do this is scanty.

The general trend since the war is that food production is increasing a little faster—but only a little faster—than population growth; but unfortunately the fastest rates of food production are in the richer territories, and the fastest rates of population increase are in some of the poorer regions. There are some considerable areas of the world where the battle is not yet being won. In some developing countries the latest reports actually show food output to be declining.

Even if in the short-term it proves possible to balance the food and population equation by increasing the supply of food at least sufficiently to match the growth of population, clearly this is no long-term solution. If there is to be any balanced equation short of wholesale decimations through war or starvation there must be an attack on the population side of the scales.

Let us very briefly recapitulate the by now well-known facts about world population.

Up to about the middle of the eighteenth century the number of people inhabiting this planet grew very slowly and at times probably was more or less stationary. Towards the end of that period it began to rise steadily but still slowly. Between 1750 and 1900 the population doubled, rising from about 750 million to 1500 million. Between 1900 and 1960 it doubled again, to 3000 million; and before the end of the century it will be 7000 million. If—and the word "if" should be stressed—the trend continues unchanged, there will be 12,000 to 13,000 million by 2025, within the lifetime of many who read this.

The experts are agreed that population trends do change, and therefore they are reserved about the more alarming predictions which suggest "standing room only" on the planet within measur-

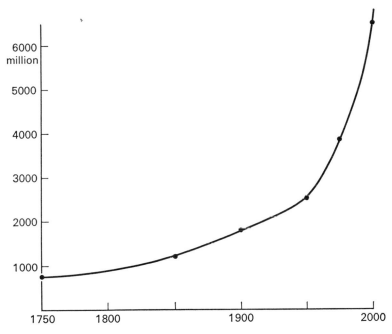

FIG. 6. Growth of world population, 1750–2000.

able time. But the immediate prospect poses sufficient of a problem, and, as we shall see, though changes in population trends do take place, they take an appreciable time to operate.

What has caused this explosion? Briefly, the success of science and medicine in keeping us alive. In the early days of the increase it was in countries like our own, where development was taking place, that growth was fastest. It is, in the final analysis, the decrease or slowing down of the death rate as compared with the more steady birth rate that raises population levels. Now it is the turn of today's developing countries to expand their numbers faster, because already, despite the limited state of some aspects of their development, science is keeping their people alive longer, and more particularly is curbing infant and child mortality.

Consider this in terms of a mother in a developing country. If, in a poor part of the world where many children die in infancy, she wants to have two or three surviving children to grow up to adulthood, she may conceive seven or eight in the knowledge that several will not survive. When improved conditions reduce the number of deaths in childhood, she will nevertheless for a period continue to bear a family of seven or eight; and perhaps six or more will now survive rather than two or three. If this trend is carried on into the next generation there will be twice or three times as many mothers now bearing children, and each of these will reproduce disproportionately large numbers as did their parents. The cumulative effect of this will not take long to show itself in the total numbers of population; and it may be two or three generations before the average family begins to reduce its size through the conscious limitation of conceptions.

The above indicates in a very rationalised and simplified form the reason why the greatest growth of population tends to come at the beginning of the development process; and of course it is not for one moment being suggested that the changes here described are the result of conscious choice. Not many parents in the conditions of early economic growth, when education and general cultural backgrounds are relatively backward, take any such deliberate decisions as we have suggested. Sheer ignorance is a far more potent cause of larger families than a mere time lag in recognising that children now remain alive that previously died; but this ignorance indeed only aggravates the situation, since it delays the time when parents do consciously redress the balance and limit their families.

The previously observed tendencies in population trends, therefore, have been:

1. A long period in which numbers remain fairly constant, because disease and famine keep the expectation of life low.
2. A comparatively short but very crucial and significant period during which growth is immensely rapid.
3. A levelling-off period because standards have risen, people have adjusted themselves to the new situation, and education and knowledge of the techniques of family planning are extended to the mass of the people.

Again we must insist that this is something of an over-simplification, and that unexpected changes in the trend do take place. Thus, one such change which does nothing to relieve the present situation is that recent trends in the developed areas of the world have been steadily upward. After a long period of declining rates which took the percentage growth of population in the developed world from 26 per cent in the first quarter of this century to 18 per cent in the second quarter, there has now been a complete turn-round, and estimates for the third quarter show a projected percentage growth of 34 per cent. This compares, however, with an estimate of 62 per cent increase for the less developed regions, so that the larger increase will be in these latter areas. Professor D. V. Glass, commenting on these figures, says:

"Much of that projected growth would occur in countries which, at present, have relatively very low levels of living. Population would grow substantially in the developed world, too, for mortality is now very low there, while fertility has in many Western countries apparently stabilised at a level considerably higher than would merely guarantee replacement. Taking the developed regions as a whole, numbers would increase by about 70 per cent between 1950 and the end of the century. In Africa, however, the medium projections imply an increase of over 150 per cent; in Asia 180 per cent; and in Latin America, over 250 per cent."

The 18 per cent increase which occurred in the developed areas between 1925 and 1950 took the population from 641 to 755 million; the less developed grew during the same period from 1266 to 1742 million, an increase of 38 per cent. In other words, the real pressure is in the developing areas.

Now, in order to understand fully the seriousness of the position, it is necessary to appreciate that, although changes do take place in population trends, they take a long time before they are effective. Even if, by whatever process, the people of the developing world were induced greatly to limit their reproduction rate (which is the technical term for their size of families), it would be a considerable time before this made very much difference to the growth of population figures. The reason is that the girls who are going to be mothers in the next thirty years are already in most cases born, and because of the present high rates of increase there are going to be far more of them at child-bearing age in ten or twenty years time than there are at the present. So not until the generation now in infancy has had a chance to grow to adulthood and to reduce its reproduction rate as compared with that of its parents can there be any effective change in trend. In those countries which now have the fastest rate of growth the proportion of young people in the population is the greatest, and hence the proportion of mothers-to-be for the next two decades is settled already at a level which is much higher than that prevailing in communities with a lower rate of increase.

To quote Professor Glass again:

"With falling mortality (the expectation of life at birth rising from 32 years in 1951 to 52 years in 1981), and with constant fertility, the total population of India would grow by some 325 millions between 1951 and 1981. *If fertility were reduced 50 per cent between 1956 and 1981, the fall beginning in 1956, population increase would certainly be much smaller. Nevertheless, growth between 1951 and 1981 would still amount to over 200 millions*" (my italics).

The implications of the population problem therefore seem fairly clear. Nothing we can do (apart from unleashing an atomic war) can prevent an enormous increase, approximately a doubling, of the world's population by the end of the century. Therefore nothing can be more important to the happiness and the peaceful existence of these human beings than to press on with all possible determination with the production of more food and other necessities, and with the whole task of development.

But in the long run life on this planet will become intolerable if not impossible unless the rising population curve can be evened out. Although there is no certainty that long-term prophecies about the likely rate of increase will necessarily be fulfilled, yet from the facts we have stated above there would seem to be every likelihood that by the time a certain stage of development has been reached and living standards in the poorer regions are making a substantial upturn there will be a levelling off of the curve.

But it is equally predictable that this levelling off will not occur for a considerable time, and that long before we can normally expect it to happen the pressure on resources, of land and food in particular, will be well-nigh unbearable.

The great name of Malthus is frequently quoted in discussions on population, and sometimes to suggest that those who prophesy doom are simply alarmists whose fears, like those of their predecessors, will prove to have been unjustified. But this is to misunderstand the Malthusian story.

Malthus maintained, at the end of the eighteenth century, that population always increased to the limit placed upon it by the productive capacities of man, and that it was futile to attempt permanently to improve the lot of mankind, because as more food was available population increased to match. As the standard of living rose, so would population grow until it bore so heavily on the food supplies that famine and illness would occur and the level of population would decline again through the shortening of average life spans; there would then be re-established, at a minimum level of subsistence, a balance between people and food.

It is claimed that this doctine has been falsified by events, because since Malthus wrote, standards in the countries of the western world have risen from above the subsistence levels which he claimed as natural, and this despite a vast growth of population. But before dismissing the Malthusian theory, it is necessary to see why this has occurred.

So far as the Europe and America of the nineteenth century were concerned, there are three main reasons for the failure of the Malthusian prophecy:

1. The expansion of the Western world enabled vast new areas of land surface to be brought into cultivation; and the great and simultaneous growth of population and living standards in the West was made possible on the ranches and prairies of North and South America, and to a lesser extent the farms and veldts of Australia and South Africa.

2. The great process of technological advance enabled there to be a much more productive use of manpower, both in industry and agriculture. In particular, it led to a much higher agricultural productivity.

3. After a certain point, as we have seen, higher standards and more education led to a levelling off of the population increase; this has, in the developed areas of the West, stabilised a situation where reasonable prosperity and affluence have been established mainly as a result of the two first-named causes.

These factors certainly disproved the truth of Malthus' theory as far as the West was concerned. But on the other side one must emphasise that this Western affluence has, in the first place, been confined as yet to a comparatively small part of the world. Secondly, it has been in considerable degree due to the cultivation of newly-discovered areas, and this is a process which by the very nature of things cannot be repeated by other continents and people. And thirdly, to some extent this affluence has been created by the exploitation of those very people who are themselves today the candidates for development.

Now, if one looks at the contemporary position of the masses now struggling towards better things in the southern continents, one finds that only one of the above three conditions may be said to apply.

Given the already huge populations in India and China, a growth rate like that which raised the numbers in England and Wales alone from 10 to 36 million in a hundred years from 1811 will result in astronomical figures. The land masses of the world, though very far from being fully utilised, do not offer any virgin soils as fertile as those superb pastures and prairies which were first put to use in the nineteenth century, and there is not remotely enough cultivable land remaining at present unused to do for these large countries and their expanding peoples what was done for the West a hundred years ago. The whole conception of a developing world such as we have envisaged leaves no room for exploitation of one people by another. We are left therefore with two factors which give some prospect of easing the situation. These are, firstly, that the technological advance which has already helped the West shall be directed towards the greater problem of aiding the impoverished countries of today. And, secondly, that the peoples of these regions may themselves, through a process of education and very radical change in their ways and habits of life, ensure that in their own case the flattening out of the population curve which has taken place in the developed countries shall begin sooner than one might expect on ground of previous experience.

What is clear is that time is not on our side, and that Malthus may yet be proved right. The whole of the second half of this book is an examination of the ways in which the first of our routes of escape may be followed, and the maximum impetus given to the technological advance. But it is equally certain that the world cannot now afford to let population trends take their course or to wait till the levelling out process follows the greater education and prosperity of the people.

A great deal is said today about the pill—the oral contraceptive pill. To many this seems a providential solution to the overpopulation problem; to others it raises vast moral issues which it would certainly be wrong to ignore.

But from the purely economic point of view, which does not concern itself with moral questions, two things must be noted.

First, the pill will certainly prove a boon to those countries which are already trying to pursue a policy of "planned population growth". Such a phrase can mean anything from programmes of persuasion by education to forced sterilisation; the development of cheap and effective means of contraception will certainly aid such plans and perhaps help to avoid the fearful prospect of compulsion.

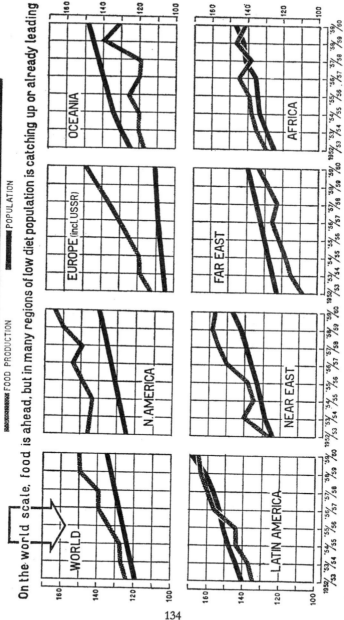

FIG. 7. (a) The race between food and population.

134

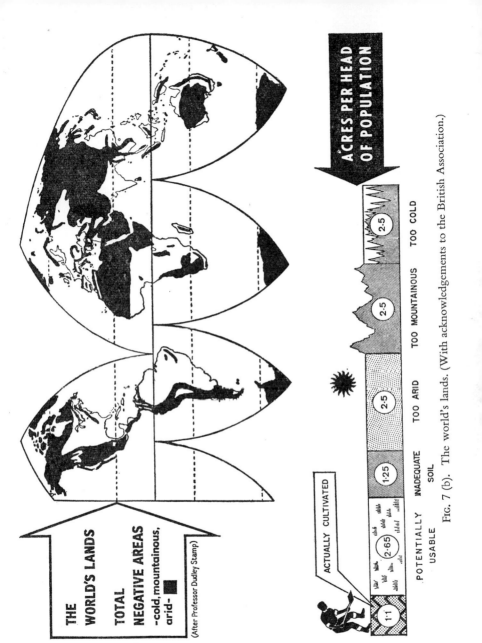

THE WORLD'S LANDS

TOTAL NEGATIVE AREAS
-cold, mountainous, arid- ■

(After Professor Dudley Stamp)

ACRES PER HEAD OF POPULATION

ACTUALLY CULTIVATED

1·1   2·65   1·25   2·5   2·5   2·5

POTENTIALLY USABLE   INADEQUATE SOIL   TOO ARID   TOO MOUNTAINOUS   TOO COLD

Fig. 7 (b).   The world's lands. (With acknowledgements to the British Association.)

On the other hand, we would be making a great mistake if we thought that use of the pill could make any difference to the food-population equation in the near future. As we have seen, changes in population rates of growth are slow to take effect; in addition, the process of educating the women of the villages of India and the jungles of the Congo in the techniques of successfully using the pill—regularly and at the right time—is likely to be a very sizeable task.

The statisticians may present their figures of doom, but the individual husband and wife will be swayed by many factors on a matter which is bound up with their most personal and intimate relations, and often with religious teachings.

But as the implications of the population explosion become more fully understood, governments begin to establish a population policy and individuals accept the need for family planning. The Roman Catholic Church itself is now in the throes of a most serious examination of the subject, following the Papal Encyclical forbidding the use of all artificial methods of family planning, including the pill. The Anglican Church has, since the Lambeth Conference of 1958, been in favour of planned parenthood, both for the family good and to solve the world problem.

The United Nations, which is neither an arbiter of morals nor a super-state, has never been able to take a firm lead in policies of population control. Its Catholic state members have prevented any decisive action in this respect. But here again the position is changing. Early in 1965 an expert was seconded by the United Nations to the Indian Government with the purpose of giving advice on population policies; previously the United Nations had contented itself with giving statistical information on population trends, but its role is now becoming more positive.

Some countries in Asia have already begun to make deliberate attempts to control the increase. In Ceylon, for example, the World Health Organisation's anti-malaria campaign was particularly successful in cutting mortality rates, reducing them by a third in two years. In the face of the increased population which this is causing Ceylon has accepted help from Sweden in a campaign to spread knowledge of family planning techniques among the people. These promise to have quite a reasonable success because there already exist quite well-developed health services, including maternity services, in the area.

Japan is the best-known example of a state which has deliberately sought to curb population growth, which between the wars was dangerously high for this island country, with its limited land area. Japan has legalised abortion and carried out an intensive educational campaign. Yet, so long does it take before a change in trend fully shows itself in statistics, that the Japanese people continue to grow in number, and will so continue at least until 1980. The rate of growth, however, has already flattened out considerably.

Mainland China, as far as one can tell, has vacillated on this issue. At times the Government has encouraged large families on the optimistic grounds that under a Marxist régime there will be enough for all; at other times they have appeared to give support to the idea of limitation.

India and Pakistan, which have some of the worst conditions, have official population limitation programmes, but at present these would seem to have made very little impact. The difficulty of persuading a largely uneducated peasant population to understand the advisability of family planning and the techniques of carrying it out is nowhere more plain than in India. Even the pill is of limited value if your community is sufficiently primitive.

Once again, one can only emphasise the personal and intimate nature of the problem. No impact will be made on it unless individual men and women, in their status as parents, can be persuaded of their own free wills that the old and often very deeply rooted desire for large families is not merely no longer necessary but is indeed against the interests of their children.

In the meantime, the urgency of proceeding with the plans for greater food production cannot be too much emphasised.

In this book we have tended to think of development as a single combined operation; and so it is. The fascinating stories of the modern scientists and agriculturists expanding the areas of food production, reclaiming the desert, irrigating the paddy fields, improving seeds, exploring the oceans for fresh supplies of fish, producing new types of food out of such substances as seaweed—these are among the finest achievements of our twentieth-century world. But they are a part of the all-round process of development; and to this process we return in the next chapter, for a final progress report.

Further Study

Background material on this subject is inexhaustible—the list grows as fast as the population.

This can be recommended. Other readable and important books are:

The World Must Eat, UNESCO Study Guide (Oceana Publications N.Y.).
The White Man's Dilemma, J. Boyd-Orr and D. Lubbock (Unwin Books).
The Population Explosion, C. W. Park (Heinemann).
The Economic History of World Population, C. M. Cipolla (Penguin).
Famine 1975, W. and P. Paddock (Wiedenfeld and Nicolson).

CHAPTER 12

The Development Decade

In Chapter 7 we outlined the growth of the U.N. aid programme from its largely unplanned beginnings to the stage where, by 1960, there at least existed a comprehensive array of instruments which could be used to speed development if the peoples and their governments had the will. But by the end of the 1950's it was clear that the progress that was being made, even allowing for all aid, not only that provided by the United Nations, was not fast enough to meet the legitimate aspirations of the poor and hungry.

Between 1950 and 1960 income per head in the developing countries rose by about 1 per cent annually; so that if your yearly income in 1950 was equivalent to $90, you might have $100 by 1960. World food supplies rose faster than population in the 1950 decade, so that there was slightly more food for each of us in the world in 1960 than in 1950. But this increase was greater in the rich countries, where we already have enough to eat; and in some of the poorer countries food hardly kept up with population.

In view of their conviction that faster growth had to be achieved, the U.N. General Assembly in 1961 passed a resolution naming the 1960's as the "Development Decade"; one hundred and four nations agreed unanimously to adopt such measures to speed development as would enable the developing countries to achieve an annual rate of growth of "aggregate national income of 5 per cent at the end of the Decade".

One thing of which we can be certain is that nobody in the United Nations seriously thought, when the Development Decade was launched, that ten years would be sufficient time for the completion of the job for which aid is being given. Even if the 5 per cent growth target should be achieved by 1970, it remains a comparatively modest one, and people will still be poor and hungry at the ends of the decade as at the beginning. But by the second half of the decade it was already becoming clear that even this modest target was not going to be reached.

The phrase "Development Decade" was coined because it was hoped that at least it would focus attention throughout the world on the whole problem of development, and that by giving targets and inviting developing nations to make plans indicating what aid they needed, there would be some approximation to a framework within which all work, U.N. and non-U.N., would find its place. Also, the targets were such as to provide each country with the opportunity of an effective start towards that moment when they can look after themselves. By 1970, even if all went well, some peoples would be ahead of their target but some would be behind; but all should be nearer take-off than when the decade began.

Having in mind population growth, 5 per cent growth of aggregate national income would mean an increase of 2 to $2\frac{1}{2}$ per cent per head, and would enable standards of living to double in twenty-five or thirty years. Twice £30 a year is £60 a year; it's not exactly luxury, and it would leave the gap between rich and poor countries proportionately the same and in absolute terms greater. But it would help to give the people of India, Africa and South America some hope and encourage them to continue their own efforts.

Such hope is urgently necessary; for without a doubt there is a growing sense of frustration in some of the newly independent nations which can lead to a hostility towards the rich and a critical world situation. A world division between north and south would be as dangerous as the more publicised east versus west differences; and it is far from unlikely unless the condition and mood of the south are relieved by a reasonable certainty of steady improvement. It could also be a more explosive division because it would be in effect a split on racial and colour lines as well as economic ones.

Paul Hoffman, the Director of the U.N. Special Fund, was one of the first to make a systematic assessment of what would be involved in the achievement of the Development Decade target. We have already quoted his statement that in the 1950's the developing countries were advancing by 1 per cent per head annually, and he points out that this rate will never provide the savings needed for capital development. He deduced that the sums needed in aid for investment must be considerably increased. Unless one is personally involved in signing government cheques for aid programmes the actual figures are not very meaningful for us, running into thousands of millions as they do; and in any case it has by now been recognised that Hoffman underestimated what would be required. But if one accepts the not illogical view that to double the rate of growth in the developing countries one needs to double the amount of aid, the position will be reasonably adequately understood and also clear in terms which all can appreciate. Put in another way, since we have already seen that we are contributing at present somewhere round about 0·6 per cent of our total product of goods and services to aid, what would be required of the developed countries would be that substantially more than 1 per cent—one pound in every hundred—should be channelled into some form of foreign aid or investment.

Hoffman insisted that this was the absolute minimum requirement if the modest targets of the Development Decade were to be reached—modest at least from the point of view of the peasant in the rice paddy field and the African villager on his tiny plot of land.

But it should be understood that this process does not go on for ever. The whole purpose of aid is to help the poorer nations to help themselves, and within a measurable period of time their own domestic resources should increase sufficiently for them to finance their own development. The more we can help now, the sooner we can stop.

In its 1961 resolution launching the Development Decade the General Assembly accepted in principle the whole conception of the Hoffman Plan, and its call for increased impetus. In the following year the U.N. Secretary-General presented to the Economic and Social Council proposals for action to be taken by the United

Nations and member governments. It is unnecessary to say much about these proposals here, because every aspect of development which has been touched on throughout this book was included. Each emerging country was recommended to produce a development plan as an action programme for the public and private sectors of its economy. The importance of trade, of capital funds made available on a long-term basis so as to allow forward planning, of agricultural and industrial development alike, of the greater application of science and technology to the backward areas were all stressed. Improvement in administration and the more systematic survey of resources were urged. Plans of action for increasing literacy and for training programmes were outlined.

Among comparatively new projects was one which, as mentioned earlier, had been a favourite of Dag Hammarskjöld, Secretary-General of the United Nations until he was killed in an air crash while visiting the Congo in 1961. This was for the United Nations to supply under technical assistance not just an expert adviser, but someone who for a time would take an actual executive role within the government of a developing country. Thus, an expert civil servant from Canada, with experience in the Ministry of Agriculture, might be seconded to Bolivia not just to advise about growing more crops or the best use to make of fertiliser, but actually to sit in a government office for twelve months and do the day-to-day work which a Permanent Secretary does under our British system. A government official from the developing country would be by his side learning the techniques of decision-making and of efficient administration; and the appropriate Minister would be receiving the daily recommendations of his internationally-provided chief officer. By 1962 there were already over two hundred requests for experts of this kind which could not be met owing mainly to shortage of funds, compared with eighty men at work under the scheme. This may be taken as a quite typical example of what happens with U.N. development work. Machinery is brought into existence to fill a growing need. Before long requests to make use of this machinery increase rapidly; but the funds available to the United Nations to meet these requests lag far behind.

This has happened with Technical Assistance, with the Special Fund, and with most U.N. agencies. The point is brought out in the same report on "Proposals for Action" when the work of the Special Fund is under consideration. It is pointed out that over half the expenditure in Fund projects is on local costs, met out of local funds; but of the remainder, of the external assistance required, it is claimed that the United Nations should be spending $250 million annually, whereas the expenditure target set by the General Assembly is only $150 million, and, since this sum is raised by voluntary contributions by governments, even this may not be reached.

In mid-1965 the Secretary-General produced a report appraising the progress made to date in the Development Decade. This is a remarkable document, because it is no dry-as-dust survey of statistical figures and committee findings. It takes a broad view, and a great deal of the whole philosophy of aid may be gleaned from its pages.

So far as the statistics are concerned, it had no very cheerful story to tell. The gap continued to widen, and the rate of growth of the developing countries actually slowed up in the first five years of the 1960's. No one reason is advanced for this, but reminding ourselves of our earlier discussions on the general theory of economic development, we may think that two factors are perhaps particularly holding back the pace of advance—firstly, the way in which the terms of trade move progressively against the poorer nations, and, secondly, the increasing burden of repayment of loans which begins now to accumulate, so that, though fresh loans may be secured, the net benefit is slight. This is a strong argument for the more frequent use of the International Development Association, with its policy of giving loans on easy terms or outright grants.

Mortality rates are thankfully going down as new health services begin to be effective, but, as we have seen, this by itself can almost be a liability unless food production increases and population planning begins to operate; and neither of these has as yet made the necessary progress. Meanwhile social changes which are allied with the general changing conditions pose other problems as men move into the towns and great slums are created and unemployment rises.

On investment, there was an indication in the 1965 report that the developed nations are not fully aware of the size of the task to which, with the rest of the world, they have committed themselves. U Thant considers that, "bemused" by their own quick responses to technical change, they have forgotten how long they themselves took to develop—from fifty to a hundred years or more. They have therefore failed to keep up the impetus of the original programmes, and their aid is barely increasing proportionately with their own growth rates; they may lend as much, but as a percentage of their national incomes it may be slightly less, and it is in no way reaching the 1 per cent plus that Paul Hoffman, and the United Nations after him, called for as a target for the developed countries.

There are few branches of human activity which are untouched by this report, since development itself, as we have seen, is an all-embracing concept. For example, in discussing the movement of population into the growing cities of the southern hemisphere, it is pointed out that "the United Nations has set targets for housing in the developing countries based on a standard of ten new dwellings for every 1,000 inhabitants. So far only two new dwellings for every 1,000 inhabitants have been built in many developing countries even though these countries have allocated 15 to 25 per cent of their total investment in capital formation to residential construction." And this reference might be paralleled in many other fields.

The halfway point, it is clear, showed many grounds for anxiety and for arguing that the efforts that are being made are as yet not enough to bridge the gap, or to increase sufficiently the basic necessities of life in proportion to the growing population.

But there is a basic note of optimism which is several times reaffirmed. For example, the value of the help and advice which developing countries are receiving from technical assistance experts, whether supplied by the United Nations, by governments, by universities or other sources, is becoming more obvious as the months and years go by. Certainly none of the now developed countries had the advantage during their formative years of the thorough surveys of needs and resources such as we have seen, for example, in the Mekong Valley scheme. And this is one of the reasons why it may be hoped that the two-thirds of the human race that has yet to go through their main growing pains will be spared some of those pains which countries like ourselves suffered.

In a more general sense, some optimism may be gathered from the very fact that the developed nations themselves were, in some cases only a few generations ago, not so far removed from the present condition of the developing. The Western Europeans, the Americans, the Russians, the Japanese, have shown that it can be done; and earlier in this book we have attempted to show some of the secrets of that development.

Though we have not attempted to go into the detailed problems of individual developing countries in the same way, we have shown that there exists no reason why they should not follow the same path; on the contrary, the international community is now happily able and organised to shoulder some of the burden. But the urgency comes—and the matter is urgent—because so many people are clamouring for better conditions at the same time. And, in the last analysis, the population figures quoted in the previous chapter supply the unchallengeable reason for us all to be concerned.

The 1965 appraisal was a document put out at a particular time to comment on a particular situation at that time; but its comments and its findings, suitably withdrawn from the context of June 1965, are likely to be valid for a good time to come. Certainly in the three years following its publication the situation has tended to get worse. It is for this reason that we have devoted considerable space to the report. We conclude this section with an extract from its last pages, which makes a plea for greater use of the international and multilateral agencies in the work of development:

"But perhaps the strongest argument for giving the international agencies a larger share in the work of development lies not so much in immediate questions of effectiveness or efficiency but in the deeper question of the kind of world community the nations are to live in. At this point it is necessary to return once more to the experience inside developed countries. When these countries confronted—as does the world to-day—the vast inequalities of wealth and opportunity which coincided with the deployment of the new resources, they did not try to bridge the gap solely by private person-to-person giving and philanthropy. The decisive change was the decision that citizens as a matter of right and social justice should begin to share more fully in the steadily increasing resources of their community. Clearly, if in the world community which science and technology are moulding into an inescapable unity, the same principles are applied, the case is very strong for an attempt to base an increasing proportion of international assistance of all sorts—in trade, in technical aid, in capital transfers, in compensatory finance—upon international institutions and upon an agreed formula or standard of obligation such as the target of 1 per cent of national income. What is formulated as a universal obligation is more likely to obviate misunderstanding and possible recriminations. What is given in the name of citizenship has the best chance of creating responsible citizens in return. This at least has been a large part of the experience of developed society in its domestic aspect. And it is still the only working experience upon which the world can draw in fashioning its own common life.

"The only experience—perhaps; but will it be used? The demands of separate, unco-operative statehood are still as vigorous as are the selfish demands of individual men and women. Yet people can rise above their cruder egoism through reason and self-interest, vision and fraternity. Is it possible for nations to be guided by the same motives? Reason tells them to-day that isolation is impossible in a world so unified in travel and communication that it is physically little more than a space ship carrying the human race through infinity. Reason and self interest tell them that if the gap between rich and poor nations can be bridged, not only will the world be happier and more peaceful, but new markets, new consumers, new opportunities for trade and investment will all be created."

Speaking to Danish students in Copenhagen in 1962, U Thant pointed out that, even with the present vast expenditure on armaments, the resources were there:

"The truth, the central stupendous truth, about developed economies to-day is that they can have—in anything but the shortest run—the kind and scale of resources they decide to have. If defence gobbles up $120 billions, the resources are provided and economies go on growing just the same. If it takes $40 billions to go to the moon, great nations will go to the moon, creating vast new electronic industries and millions of new jobs, products and opportunities as they go. It is no longer resources that limit decisions. It is the decision that makes the resources. This is the fundamental revolutionary change—perhaps the most revolutionary mankind has ever known."

It is revolutionary because economists have always described economics as the study of human activity in making use of scarce resources which can be put to alternative uses; and the emphasis has been on the word "scarce". It is because of scarcity in relation to demand that things have value, and one has to plan the allocation of one's resources between different uses. If U Thant is right—and whatever exaggeration there may be in his words, there is a staggering truth about them—the element of choice still remains, but we no longer have to worry so much about the scarcity of resources. We can go to the moon; but we can also, if we will it, eliminate poverty. From the viewpoint of the African peasant working still with his antiquated tools in the hot sun for a mere subsistence this may seem a far-fetched dream; but from the Secretary-General's office on the top floor of the New York headquarters of the United Nations there is a different view; and one which is changing, albeit slowly, the viewpoint of the African peasant.

Further Study

A continuing interest in the progress of international aid and U.N. programmes is clearly the only possible follow-up to the subject of this chapter. The U.N. Information Centre will mail progress reports to interested individuals or groups.

The relevant documents on which the chapter is based are:

The United Nations Development Decade—Proposals for Action.

United Nations Development Decade at Midpoint (1965). (This is available as a pamphlet from the U.N. Association.)

CHAPTER 13

Back to People

WE should end where we began—with people. In the last resort the development plans of the nations will be carried out by tens of millions of people, individuals working in their fields, with their boats, in the new factories and mills, on the rubber plantations and in the home.

But we should stop thinking about tens of millions. All that we have been discussing—population, river valley developments, education—is about individual people, single families living together in poverty, whose poverty may be edged over the border-line to starvation if another child is born and lives, whose hardships may be lightened if they can be shown how to plan their families.

Yet to do this, as we have said earlier, involves an interference with some of the most intimate concerns of every human being. And if this relation between the worldwide statistical issues about which economists and politicians argue and the tradition-hallowed behaviour and daily life of the fisherman in Chile and the villager in India is most obvious when we consider population problems, yet it is always there—in every economic plan, in every social reform, in every resolution passed by the United Nations.

So this survey should conclude with a few thoughts not so much about the effect of economic development on people but rather with the effect of people on economic development; for if the people do not want development it will not come, or if it comes it will be in a less agreeable form.

It may be argued that everyone wants more food, more prosperity, a higher standard of living, a chance to be educated, to live long and richly.

This is true; but it is also true that everyone wants peace, yet we have wars. The fact is that too often we do things which are not compatible with peace; human beings may want peace, but human behaviour takes, maybe unwittingly, some form which leads to war.

Similarly, the putting into operation of all the fine schemes for economic growth and development involves all of us in a change of mental attitude and behaviour which is sometimes quite unpalatable. Old ways of living which have gone on for centuries, and which are rooted in the whole custom and tradition of a society, may have to be altered. Are those who are asked to change in this way willing to do so?

There is here, as so often, a tension which has to be appreciated and resolved by every person who is concerned with development— and particularly by the technical experts and others who come directly into contact with the people of the developing countries. This tension is between the need for change and the resistance to it caused by habit and tradition.

There are those who, faced with this tension, take one or other of the extreme views. They may say "Then leave people alone; if they don't want to change, don't make them." There are two reasons why this attitude is untenable.

Firstly, because resistance to change may often be due to ignorance, or to having lived so long in hopeless conditions that when hope does come there is no response to it. Secondly, there is no lack of desire for change among the leaders of the developing countries, who are in general those who have seen the possibility of better things and realise the need for an improvement. They are determined that something shall be done.

On the other side there are those who want to brush aside objections and resistances, and to make the Plan go through at all costs. This attitude, too, is to be fought, since a failure to do so can only mean that projects and targets—abstract things—are being given priority over people. The Mekong Valley scheme is not, like Mount Everest, something to be tackled "because it is there", but because it will affect the existence and well-being of the families and communities who live in this region.

To strike a balance between these two extremes is not easy, but it must be done.

The ability to understand the reasons why people who need help sometimes refuse it and even object to its offer is one of the most necessary and valuable assets for anyone who works with other people. Every social worker, trying to find suitable accommodation for an old couple, or a job for a released prisoner, or to help teen-agers in trouble, knows the need for this ability. And equally in development work this same social instinct is vital.

It leads one to understand why, when people have been shown that new ways are better they nevertheless may revert to old ones. It leads one to see that the reason may be that they have been so used to poverty that they have no energy to change their habits because change means effort. It shows that, in Gunnar Myrdal's phrase, the very poor do no more than "set their sights on survival"; and, if this is the case, they cannot be expected to see the stars.

An officer who comes to tell a village new ways of cultivating their land or looking after their cattle gives them his advice and then, after a time, leaves the place. If his ideas are wrong, if something fails to work, the villagers, who remain, may die.

It has been found that in some of the literacy campaigns which have been carried out by UNESCO and other agencies, splendid results have apparently been achieved, but a year later nearly every-one has forgotten again how to read. This is because there seems no meaning in literacy to them; their lives have been lived around a world so arranged over generations as to avoid the necessity for reading.

Again, let it be emphasised that this does not mean that to teach literacy to primitive peoples is unnecessary; because so long as they remain illiterate they remain primitive. But it does mean that development is a unitary process, and neither food nor health nor technical aid nor literacy can be treated as a separate thing; all must be regarded as part of a whole.

The realisation of this fact, and of the necessity to change minds before conditions can be changed fundamentally, has led to the concept of Community Development. The best-known example of this is the big programme launched by the Indian Government soon after independence. It was inspired by the ideas and ideals of Gandhi, who saw that in a country of 550,000 villages it was the villager who ultimately mattered most. You must persuade him that a little elementary education for his children will give them a fuller life and greater opportunity; you must teach his womenfolk the value in happiness and health which comes from practising the simplest hygiene; you must encourage him to share the use of a farm tractor with others in the village, since no one can afford his own; you must in short build up a community of people working together for mutual help.

The Community Development programme establishes the "panchayat" as the democratic village council which is responsible for a great deal of the decisions and planning in the village. Villages are combined into administrative groups of about a hundred, and can call on professional advisers in social education, co-operation, agricultural methods and many other things.

This grass-roots programme means that, as the major development projects of the Indian Government's Five-Year Plans get under way, there should be in the villages a growing sense of participation in the national effort, and an acquisition of the simple basic skills, including the vital skill of self-government, which will enable the people to use the irrigation works and to operate the newly-established village industries.

It is an imaginative idea being worked out by many devoted officials. It should be of particular interest to us in the West because it is the greatest attempt as yet by one of the poorest of all states to develop systematically by a process which is essentially democratic.

As to its success, there are many voices; and probably it is as yet too early to give judgement. The general impression obtained from observers who have seen the panchayat in operation is that, though the scheme is alive and has achieved much, the hopeless grind of the daily battle against starvation still leaves most of the villagers apathetic; it may be true that it is easier to build a steel plant than to change a man's mind.

There are villages where a great deal of progress has been made; and it is notable that where something has already been achieved there may be a willingness to do more, because hope has been nourished by a modest success. But too often the bad old customs remain. The irrigation channels have been dug, but the farmers do not use them. Landlords, who do not work on their land, see no point in mechanisation in order to make life easier for their labourers. Purdah continues and the women remain a backward race, apart. When a young man is educated, he will no longer work on the land and is removed in attitude and way of life from his elders.

One acute Indian observer who spent a long period touring the whole country summed up that change and development must depend on the desire of the community for a rising standard, and probably the majority of the rural people are against change because of the effort involved. Yet there are exceptions which show the possibilities; and one of the most encouraging messages is that where there is a panchayat consisting of younger men and women it does get things done and have a more progressive outlook.

Nowhere else is there such an elaborate plan of community development as in India; but more and more countries and aid-giving agencies are seeing its importance and are recognising that development must mean finding a way which will involve acceptance by the individual peasant and his family. One must work with people, rather than for people. Mr. T. R. Batten, among whose tasks as Supervisor of Development Studies at London University it has been for many years to train men and women from the developing countries for social and community work at home, has stressed that often the best workers would be village people themselves who were just literate, rather than the graduate who because of his education has lost touch with the grass-roots level.

Sometimes, of course, the villager, the "local", may be wiser than the expert. The latter may have forgotten, for example, that if you use a deep plough you may break up the land and cause soil erosion unless your whole method of agriculture changes with the introduction of the plough. If a man chooses to work less and to rest more than seems necessary, he may be right. He may know the climatic conditions better than a stranger; and, in any case, why should he not choose his way of life?

There is, indeed, an interchange of minds and traditions which can benefit both sides. The world of ulcers and coronaries, of pep pills and nervous breakdowns, may have a good deal to learn from the other civilisations. Only of one thing can we be quite sure; that no one goes hungry by choice, and no one willingly sees his or her child suffer if relief is known to be possible.

It is not only in the villages and the rural areas that one has to take note of local conditions. One can learn from *The Japanese Factory*, by James C. Abbeglen, of the errors which can be made if one regards Japanese industry as a mere replica of Western. Because the social system of Japan is different from ours, their industrial organisation is different.

Thus, the essential relationship of owner to employee in an English or American factory is contractual—one man undertakes to work for another on agreed conditions. There is no bond or obligation between them except that of keeping each to his side of the contract.

But Japanese society retains a great deal of the paternalism of the feudal state from which Japan has only quite recently emerged. The factory management regards itself as having something of the relationship of the head of a family to its employees; one result of this is that Japanese firms very rarely fire their workers. They will keep them on in some job which may be very much of a sinecure, and as a result the factory may suffer from over-employment. On the other hand, the worker feels himself a member of a group which includes the management, and he receives very considerable benefits and bonuses which help to maintain his loyalty to the undertaking.

It follows from this that any attempt to introduce high-pressure American methods of business organisation may be quite unsuited to the Japanese social order. By American standards an undertaking might be inefficient and would gain much from a wholesale pruning of staff and job evaluation. But a great deal of the success of the Japanese in reaching such a high level of development so soon may well be due to the fact that, by retaining their traditional social relationships and adapting them to industrialisation, they have avoided some of the disruptions and tensions which are found in some other societies. It is not a question of which is the best way; it is rather a question of which fits a particular community best at a particular time.

A book, rather than a section of a chapter, might be written on this general theme because it is so fundamental. But enough has been said, one hopes, to make it clear that in the last resort development stands or falls on the grounds of the quality of human relationships. As we said at the very beginning of this book, we are concerned here with the social sciences, and in the social sciences there are not straight categorical answers. You devise a plan to make the best uses of your resources, whatever these may be in a particular situation; but your greatest, most unique, most essential resource is always the human being; and the human being is not just a machine, but something which feels, something which has grown up and shaped itself within a particular society to which it belongs. One can only assist people, whether individuals or whole groups and societies, if one works with them.

The changes which come in the wake of development, then, need very considerable adjustments in the minds of all—the people of the developed as much as those of the developing countries. In particular it is necessary that anyone who goes from a country like England on some form of activity associated with this work, whether it be a technical assistance expert, a worker in a British firm overseas, or an international service volunteer, must appreciate the special psychological difficulties which he may meet—the suspicion that may exist of the white man, the clinging to old habits and customs because these afford the only security and certainty that an illiterate and poverty-stricken Indian or African may know; the completely different attitude on many fundamentals which may exist and which make misunderstanding easy and true partnership terribly difficult, the resentment of any suggestion of an implied superiority on the part of any giver of aid.

He must realise more particularly the world of difference in ideas, in religious beliefs, in the whole life and customs of society

which sometimes exist between himself and the people with whom
he is working. A distinguished international civil servant who for
over a quarter of a century has been engaged in technical assistance
has said that only during the last few years of that time did he begin
to realise fully the overriding importance of attempting to understand the social pattern and the psychology of those with whom he
was dealing. The distinction between the cow as an economic unit
which can give milk and meat and the cow as a sacred animal
which has spiritual, but not economic, value is just one example of
the way in which outlooks can vary. The different approaches to the
position of children and old people in the community illustrate the
kind of attitude which should be known by anyone who is venturing
to give service to an underdeveloped community; and, of course,
the status of women in the society.

So, when we say that development depends on people, we mean
all people—not only on the work and will of those in the developing
countries today, but also on the understanding and compassion of
those in the developed.

Whatever the reasons for the pre-eminence of the West in
industrialisation and technology and in standards of living up to the
present time, there can be no doubt that we living in the West today
find ourselves in a privileged position because of no credit to ourselves as individuals. The standard we enjoy is due to the scientists
and technologists and businessmen of the eighteenth and nineteenth centuries, the factory workers who toiled and starved in
building up English industrial prosperity, and the Asian coolies
and African natives whose exploitation brought more wealth to
Europe.

In the "Welfare State" to which all British political parties are
now committed, it is accepted that the community as a whole has
a responsibility to assist those of its members who have, perhaps
temporarily, fallen on hard times, such as sickness or unemployment,
or who, like old people, are unable to fend for themselves. It has
been generally agreed that this not only satisfies our conceptions of
justice and fair play, but also pays off in terms of prosperity through
the improved health of the community, the extra productivity and

the maintenance of purchasing power and full employment, and in many other ways.

The world-size matters which we have been considering in these pages may in one sense be regarded as the extension of these principles of the welfare state to the world as a whole. There is no doubt that, in the long run, the prosperity of ourselves and our children in this country is bound up with the prosperity of the rest of the world, including those parts which are now poor; and this self-interest coincides with that instinctive sense of compassion and sympathy which has led so many of the British public to contribute so willingly to causes like the Freedom from Hunger Campaign, and so many young people to volunteer for service overseas. But, as this book has tried to show, you cannot solve the world's problem of poverty by charity or even by voluntary service. The job needs the conscious participation of all of us, and perhaps more than anything else an intelligent understanding of the basic principles and issues involved. This generation sometimes seems obsessed with the kind of death wish which is causing some governments to direct that every house-holder must have his air-raid shelter—a shelter, mark you, to be effective in the days of the H-bomb, not merely of the conventional high-explosive weapons which accounted for hundreds of thousands of victims in one night over Dresden in the last war. This is the kind of foolishness which is only committed by those whose minds cannot move forward, who in the 1960's still think of national wars and narrow diplomacies. To them any talk of real co-operation across frontiers, between people of different races and skins, is idealistic, visionary and unpractical. But it is they who are un-practical. The truly practical men and women today are the men and women of the U.N. agencies, whether planning at their head-quarters or at work in the field, together with all those others who have realised the truth of Toynbee's statement that this age could be the first in which people everywhere understood that they could combine their resources in a common fight against mankind's real enemies. For the fact is—the practical fact—that we have the know-ledge and the power to succeed in this undertaking.

Further Study

There are ways in which groups in this country can make direct contact with groups in developing countries abroad. Teachers who are seconded for a spell to an African or Asian country may like to keep a link with their home town or school. The latter can be of practical help in providing books and other material.

Oxfam, War on Want, UNESCO (through their Gift Coupon scheme) can all help a group to choose a particular project which they can aid, and from this can see the progress of a specific scheme. Such help, if planned by one of the recognised bodies such as those mentioned, is never just charity, but is always in the true meaning aid for development, designed to help the underdeveloped to help themselves. Involvement in such a project teaches more of the problems and achievements of aid than anything else, because it brings us "back to people".

Index